THE APOLOGETICS OF EVIL

PRINCETON MONOGRAPHS
IN PHILOSOPHY

Harry G. Frankfurt, Editor

————————————— •¶M℗• —————————————

The Princeton Monographs in Philosophy series offers short
historical and systematic studies on a wide variety
of philosophical topics.

THE APOLOGETICS
OF EVIL

THE CASE OF IAGO

Richard Raatzsch

Translated from the German by Ladislaus Löb

PRINCETON UNIVERSITY PRESS

PRINCETON AND OXFORD

Library of Congress Cataloging-in-Publication Data

Raatzsch, Richard.
The apologetics of evil : the case of Iago / Richard Raatzsch ;
translated from German by Ladislaus Löb.
p. cm. — (Princeton monographs in philosophy)
Includes bibliographical references and index.
ISBN 978-0-691-13733-9 (acid-free paper)   1. Shakespeare, William,
1564–1616—Characters—Iago.   2. Shakespeare, William, 1564–1616.
Othello.   3. Evil in literature.   I. Title.
PR2993.I3R33 2009
822.3′3—dc22   2008040961

British Library Cataloging-in-Publication Data is available

This book has been composed in Janson Typeface

Printed on acid-free paper. ∞

press.princeton.edu

Printed in the United States of America

1   3   5   7   9   10   8   6   4   2

Contents

THE APOLOGETICS OF EVIL

Introduction

1. If there is any reason why Iago is called "Iago" (and not "Othello," "Cassio," or whatever else), it could be because of the resemblance between the word "Iago" and the word "ego." For just as the word "ego" is connected with the concept of egoism, contemplation of Iago's actions, too, leads to a concept—the concept of Iago—which resembles the concept of egoism.

For many people, calling someone an egoist is a way of criticizing him morally. However, some of those who think and speak that way also agree that egoism is a more or less natural stance of humans who, as living individuals, just have to take care of their own well-being or at least of their survival. If, however, this is true, how can one criticize someone morally for being an egoist, except by using the word in a different, although related sense—and so by being the victim of some kind of confusion? However, some people, mostly philosophers, would be inclined to say that there is not only nothing morally wrong about being an egoist, but that, properly understood, egoism is the real basis of morality. If egoism is indeed our natural stance toward one another, which other natural basis could morality possibly have? And if morality did not have a natural basis, how could it ever have come into being, or, even if it did somehow arise, how could it ever persist? Is morality, in the end, nothing but a chimera? This is the place where one might feel tempted to bring in Iago. Even if the egoist, the argument goes, may be in general more or less morally acceptable, an Iago is *definitely* not. If there is any *unconditional* evil in the world, then "Iago" is its name.

Or so it seems.

2. This study consists of two parts: first a discussion of the concept of Iago, then an apologia for Iago. Questions about the proper order in which the discussion should proceed are often of substantive importance in philosophical reflection. In our case, however, this order is not as obvious as it might seem to be. The reason for this is that the distinction on which it is based is itself less self-evident than is generally assumed. To proceed as I propose to do has the distinct advantage of making it clear that the "apologia" which I will present in the second part of this essay refers not to Iago as a person or an individual literary character, but to a certain concept that we derive from studying him and his actions, and that we may also call by his name.

It could be argued that Iago cannot actually correspond to his concept on the ground that "Iago" is a proper name, and a proper name is not a concept. In general this is true, but in Iago's case things are somewhat more complicated.

"Iago" is the name of a character in Shakespeare's play *Othello*. "Othello" is also a proper name, the name of a character in a Shakespearean play of the same name. The word "Othello" is thus the name both of a character and of a play.

That one and the same name is the proper name of more than one individual is nothing unusual. A brief glance at the telephone directory of any sizable town shows countless proper names referring to more than one person. That two individuals have the same name is often no more than a coincidence. It could easily have been different. In this sense the fact that Shakespeare's play *Othello* is called *Othello* is also a coincidence. *Othello* could just as well have been called *Iago*. Iago and Othello could have answered to each other's name, at least within certain limits. But then everything is valid only within certain limits or on certain occasions.

Perhaps the play *should* have been called *Iago* rather than *Othello*. After all, it is probably Iago who leaves the sharpest, strongest, most lasting impression of all the characters. (In this respect Iago is in no way inferior to Othello.) But if the play were called *Iago* for that reason, it would no longer be a coincidence. From this perspective, of course, it is no coincidence either that it is in fact called *Othello*. To test these assertions, let us assume that we found the text among Shakespeare's unpublished works, without a title. In that case, would it not have been only natural to call it *Othello* or possibly *Iago* or, at a pinch, *Desdemona*, but certainly not *Roderigo*, even though the last two are characters in the play? And now compare this to a case in which we ask what name should *naturally* be given to an infant who has as yet no name. Here, with the exception of quite special cases, we do not even know what that is supposed to mean.

This is related to a distinction I have just made in passing, which was blurred when I spoke of the word

"Othello" as being both the name of a character in a play and the name of the play itself. The difference is that between "Othello" as the name of Othello and *Othello* as the title of the play (in which Othello appears). With reference to certain persons, "Othello," "Cassio," and "Iago" are not titles, while "General," "Lieutenant," and "Ancient" (i.e., "Ensign") definitely are. But these three words, again, are not titles in the same sense in which *Othello* is the title of a play by Shakespeare. There are many generals, even more lieutenants, and countless ensigns, but only one play *Othello*. This could be safely asserted even if de facto there were several plays with that title. For the meaning is clear: of Shakespeare's *Othello* there is only one specimen, and if there were more (by Shakespeare) either they would be variants of each other or the case would resemble that of two individuals with the same proper name: it would be pure coincidence. In this sense of "coincidence," however, it is *no* coincidence if two men are lieutenants. The urge to find out why two or more plays bear the same title, even though they definitely do not look like variants of each other, reveals the significance of any case that does involve variants: for when we try to discover the reason for the homonymy, we are looking for a link between the named entities. In so doing we are looking for a point of view that would allow us to consider them as variants of each other. That again refers back to the fact that a play is rarely called what it is called by pure coincidence.

Talking of point of view, there is a sense in which people, too, are generally called what they are called not by coincidence, but for one of a variety of reasons. If we describe it as a coincidence that "James Jones" is called what he is called, we mean that, given the kind of person

James Jones is, he would not necessarily have to be called "James Jones." Contrary to the impression I may have created, this is not down to James Jones alone. It is also due to the total lack of clarity as to what James Jones would have to be like if we were to say that he has the name that exactly fits him. *Nomen est omen* is a useful saying precisely because it is not universally valid; this means that when it *does* apply, this is a *significant* feature of the situation. Nevertheless, in countless cases we know virtually nothing about a person if we know only his name. Usually the connection between who a person is and what he is called is only an external one. If it were different, how could *some* names move us in a peculiar way? In contrast, the connection between a title and a play is not merely an external one.

The fact that Othello bears his name by coincidence, while Shakespeare's play is not called *Othello* coincidentally, does not leave Othello himself untouched. Rather, it endows him with a special status. Othello is not simply an individual like any other. The play is not a factual report like a weather report or the police report of a crime. No play is, not even a historical one. There is a sense in which Othello is exemplary. However, the prime reason for this is not that the play in which he appears is called *Othello*. Rather, it is primarily because he lives in a play, and then perhaps a little because of the name of this play. Given that Othello's life in this play, in comparison to that of the other characters, looks as it does, and given many other things, it is not surprising that the play is named after him. The starting point, however, is still his paradigmatic status, his exemplariness. To say that something is exemplary or a paradigm, does not, of course, necessarily imply a positive moral judgment on it. One can

speak of a "paradigm case" or a "good exemplar" of stock
market fraud, road rage, or child abuse without suggest-
ing that any of these are anything but evil. The same as
with regard to Iago applies to some degree to all the other
characters, who are also part of the play. However, their
exemplariness is placed in the service of Othello more
than his is in theirs.

With one exception, of course: Iago. As I have said before, he is the most memorable and exciting character
in the play. In line with the intended effect of the play,
his status as a paradigm is perhaps even more pronounced
than Othello's. And if the less exemplary figure is set side
by side with the most paradigmatic, Othello serves Iago,
rather than the reverse. In this respect Iago would be the
general.

What matters is the exemplariness; for it is the exemplariness of the individual called "Iago" that aligns his
name with a concept. To that extent "Iago" may be said
to be not simply the name of a person, but the name of a
person who embodies a concept. "Iago" is a proper name
and at the same time the name of a concept. It is the name
of the character in the play, but because the character
exists only in the play, he personifies something general,
that is, a concept. That is why we can first discuss the concept of Iago, before we move on to the apologia of Iago;
this assumes, of course, that one can give the apologia of
something general, such as a concept.

3. These observations, then, follow a deliberate pattern:
first comes the concept and then an apologia. One exception to this order is section 7, which contains a brief summary of the whole study. Since it is a summary, it could
have come just as well at the end as at the beginning. Why

it is where it is should become clear at that particular point.

Contrary to appearances, the sequence concept-then-apologia is by no means obvious. Naturally, at first sight it looks as if there could be no other way of proceeding than by saying what the apologia is for, before attempting the apologia itself. But a little reflection will soon make us unsure that this order is always appropriate. There are times when we really do not know *what* (or *who*) it is that we are talking about even if we know *how* we are appraising it (or him or her); just as at other times, once we have understood the nature of some things (or some persons), we hardly understand what we thought we were doing when we tried to justify or to defend them. Iago himself is a striking example of this.

Naturally, in order to be able to defend or to justify something—both the difference and the connection between the two activities will be discussed in more detail below—we need first to know what that something is. But the word "first" as used here does not mean that the thing in question is necessarily independent of our evaluation of it. Nor does it mean that understanding the thing must be logically prior to evaluating it. If I want to undertake a pilgrimage to Rome, I must first make a start. But this does not make my start independent of my pilgrimage; rather, the start is part of the pilgrimage, which in its turn consists of the start and my further actions. Even if the relationship between facts and values is not of the same kind as that between the start and the pilgrimage, still the concept-then-apologia sequence will be warranted only to the extent that the subject matter itself is independent of, or logically prior to, its value. But to what extent is it that?

To determine that extent would be to mediate between the clear and obvious statement that the concept comes first—that is, before the apologia—and the reservations that might result from reflecting on specific cases. This entails neither that we ought simply to regard that statement as a model of how things are, nor that we ought simply to share those reservations. Rather, both together should lead us to wonder whether in some domains a definition that does not contain some sort of valuation is no definition at all. One further consideration also points in this direction: it is not clear how far it is possible really to understand the play without developing some fairly clear-cut moral feelings about Iago, although it also cannot be said that having these feelings alone proves that one has understood the play fully. The evocation of certain feelings need not be what everything in the drama depends on or aims at. This does not, however, in itself mean that those feelings lack all importance.

In any case, the vacillation to which we easily succumb when faced with the question about the (supposed) independence or the (missing) primacy of a thing in relation to its value is reflected in my presentation by the continuous numbering of the individual sections, which signals the unity of the argument, and the division into chapters, which partly contradicts it.

4. In what follows, then, Iago matters only insofar as he instantiates and defines a concept (his own). Given what Iago is like, the question of ethics immediately arises. Since an apologia is a value-oriented enterprise, the term "Apologetics" almost immediately suggests itself as a title of our inquiry. But ethics and drama are different things, at least if we think of something like *Othello* when we

hear the word "drama." How, then, could a *drama*, of all things, best represent the concept of Iago by supplying a model for him?

The difference between drama and ethics implies the independence of one from the other. This, however, tells us nothing about the exact nature and meaning of the difference and consequently of the independence. An engine and a crankshaft are different things, albeit not different things of the same kind. But ethics and drama are certainly not two different things in the same way as an engine and a crankshaft are. Nor are they two different things in the same sense as beetroot and music. Rather, drama and ethics are connected in essence, without either being part of the other. This relationship expresses itself in the various ways in which we react to plays. For instance, in order to test whether someone has understood a play we often ask him to articulate its "moral." It does not necessarily matter that the moral can be seen differently by different spectators, even if they are members of the same "moral community." The fact that the same thing can be seen differently does not mean that it can be seen in any way one wishes—or that if it can be seen in any way one wishes, any view of it must be a moral one. (Incidentally, this is one reason why I am not claiming to provide *the* interpretation of *Othello* here. This is true regardless of the fact that "moral" means different things to different people. For us it is enough that the uses of this term, despite their diversity, show *some* coherence.) On the other hand, ethical systems seem to have no more content than can be indicated by a description of the difference it would make if they were to be transferred to real life. And why should it not be possible to act these out? Which obviously brings us back to the drama itself.

Ethics and drama, then, appear to be simply two sides of the same coin, with the play as an ethical counterpart, created for adults, of what was exemplified in formal terms by the mother who showed her child some greeting cards, saying, "Now you know what bad taste is."[1] But of course it is not as simple as that. Or rather, the idea that it is as simple as that is met by an obstacle.

> "You were witnesses. What did you see?"
> A: "I saw the accused stabbing the victim with a knife."
> B: "I saw evil."

We would not accept B's statement lightly and without further discussion. But if the moral is not visible, how could a drama be an object lesson in ethics? After all, we would not say, or at least not without further thought, that being presented onstage is a mere external appendage to the events in question and does not touch their essence.

If this question can be answered at all satisfactorily, then certainly not here. However, that is a serious deficiency only if we allow the differences between drama and ethics to make us lose sight of the connection between them; in other words, if we fall victim to prejudice. But if the stress is placed on the connection, as it is here, the neglect of the difference will not be a grave problem, particularly if attention is drawn to it, as it is now.

---

[1] The example is taken from Oswald Hanfling, "Learning about Right and Wrong: Ethics and Language," *Philosophy* 78 (2003): 25–41. See also Elizabeth Wolgast, "Moral Paradigms," *Philosophy* 70 (1995): 143–55.

Chapter One

The Concept of Iago

1.1. The Origin of the Concept

5. At the beginning, it was suggested that the reason why Iago is called "Iago" could be the resemblance between this name and the word "ego." An egoist is said to be a person whose first—or only—thought is always of himself. Thus egoism is, above all, the attitude and the concomitant behavior of a person who believes that he always comes first or that he is the only thing that matters. Others therefore only come second or are irrelevant (even though they have a fundamental importance for the egoist, as will be explained later). Accordingly, Iago might lend his name to an attitude like that of the egoist, but deviating from it in some important points. There is a sense in which Iago is an egoist raised to an absolute level and therefore no longer just an egoist. Exactly what that means is the topic of this study.

6. A few reminders of *Othello* may bring the picture of Iago—and therefore the concept of Iago—before our eyes in somewhat more vivid outlines.

Iago is the ensign of Othello, a general in the service of the Venetian Republic. Situated in the hierarchy between Iago and his general is the lieutenant Cassio. Othello and Iago are married to Desdemona and Emilia, respectively. Cassio is single but probably has a mistress. Apart from these, only one other character has a sizable role: Roderigo, a Venetian nobleman, who is in love with Desdemona.

In a nutshell, the plot of the play is as follows: Iago hatches a plan, tangentially involving Roderigo, to make Othello jealous of Cassio. The plan succeeds to the extent that Othello orders Iago to murder Cassio. However, when the order is carried out, it is Roderigo who is killed, and Cassio is merely wounded. Othello strangles Desdemona and—once Emilia reveals the truth about Iago's plot—he kills himself. Thereupon, Iago stabs Emilia and is arrested, while Cassio is appointed general in Othello's place.

7. Why, then, is the play called *Othello* and not *Iago* (or at least *Othello and Iago*)? To anticipate my conclusion: Calling the play *Iago* would contradict what I believe to be its meaning. My own interpretation contends that Iago is a character whose actions cannot be justified but can be defended. The risk involved in this formulation is the ease with which it can be misunderstood—*Aside, sotto voce*: Iago is a character whose actions cannot be justified; but *aloud, to the audience*: they can nevertheless be defended. That Iago, or his actions, cannot be justified would seem to go without saying. But can he be defended, all the same? This could easily give the impression that the unexpected part of my analysis, the defense, is the main thing, and the obvious part, the impossibility of justifi-

cation, is a minor matter. From this impression it is not
far to the thesis that the play is really a glorification of
Iago, a paean to ruthlessness, a song of praise for incon-
siderateness raised to an absolute level. In order really
to be considerate, rather than just feigning this virtue, we
must be aware that others also have a claim to be considered, and we must acknowledge this claim. This is precisely what is not true of Iago. One might then think
that the play is merely a celebration of the active principle
in the human species, realized in a single individual who
knows no limitations apart from those of natural necessity
and destiny. However, since the play is called *Othello*, this
does not appear to be a very promising line of interpretation. Nevertheless, the play makes it rather visible that
the connections between Iago and Othello, the two main
protagonists, are internal ones—as the relation between
the two sides of one and the same coin is an internal relation. The fact that Iago is the dominating figure in a
play which is called *Othello*, or the tension between content and title, if you like, should focus the spectator's, or
reader's, attention on the *complexity* of the moral situation. Therefore, to ask whether the play simply praises
or simply condemns ruthlessness is too simple a question.
The real moral situation is more complex than these questions allow it to be. That is, there is indeed an element
of a praise of ruthlessness in the play; it is, however, not
a form of praise that is simply the opposite of a condemnation of ruthlessness. One can see that the questions
asked above are too simple by reflecting that the only
appropriate answer to them would be that the play is a
form of condemning praise, or a praising condemnation,
of ruthlessness.

1.2. ACTING WITHOUT A MOTIVE?

8. In section 6 I gave a brief summary of the action of *Othello*, providing a pattern for an ostensive definition of the concept of Iago. Is anything essential missing in that pattern? Yes and no. Naturally, one thing that is missing is what Othello asks Cassio about, when the complete panorama of Iago's actions is revealed to him:

> Will you, I pray, demand that demi-devil
> *Why* he hath thus ensnar'd my soul and body?
>
> $(5.2.302-3)^1$

What is missing is Iago's motive, the force that drives all his actions, unites them into a whole, and supplies them with a content. The absence of a visible, strong enough motive might easily appear to be an essential or fatal defect, because, as Samuel Johnson says, "nothing is essential to the fable but unity of action."² However, why must unity of action presuppose a single, unifying motive? Are not more complex and unusual forms of unity of action dramatically possible?

The unity of action of which Johnson speaks is the unity in the multiplicity of those deeds that constitute the play. The sequence of scenes that make up a play, at least in its old-fashioned forms, is essentially different from the sequence of scenes we see, for example, if we zap from one television program to the next, even if all the chan-

---

¹ W. Shakespeare, *Othello*, ed. M. R. Ridley, New Arden Edition (London: Methuen, 1958). Quotations follow the pattern "act.scene.line(s)." The emphasis is mine.

² S. Johnson, *The Plays of William Shakespeare* (1765), in *Samuel Johnson: A Critical Edition of the Major Works*, ed. D. Greene, The Oxford Authors (Oxford: Oxford University Press, 1984), pp. 432f.

nels happen to be showing soap operas, which are all more or less alike. This, too, could create a certain unity and could even be intended to do so, but, as a kind of parody of traditional drama, it shows that the original unity of scenes envisaged by Johnson is of a different kind. This unity of a complex but unified action, mutatis mutandis, also applies internally to the actors involved. Each of them, or at any rate each of the main characters, must have a visibly unified motivational structure.

The complex action that constitutes a play is the result of the combination, opposition, and jumble of characters. In this process the characters themselves reveal a certain unity. In fact, dramatic characters are more than just figures who pop up, looking more or less unchanged and bearing the same name, in several scenes. Rather, it is a certain unity expressed by what these figures do that allows us to call them characters to start with. In establishing this unity for a character such as Iago, the question of motive is of central importance. Even if we can name a motive for each of the many actions of Iago, there still remains the question why he undertakes this set of actions as *a whole*.

There is a sense in which only a response to this question will allow us to answer our original questions. If a person opens a window in order to lower the temperature in the room, we know why he opens the window; therefore we understand what he is doing. But what if he is trying to lower the temperature in the room because in the cot there is a naked baby who preempts his claim to an inheritance? Would we still want to say with the same straightforward simplicity that we know why he is doing what he is doing as he opens the window, because we know that he wants the room to be as cold as possible?

And that he has sent the nanny away in order to prevent her closing the window? And so on.

However, the question what motive really drives Iago is not easy to answer. This is a remarkable fact. Indeed it is even more remarkable than is normally the case when the motives of the actors are unclear, either in a play or in real life. In recognition of the importance of this fact, it is both helpful and necessary to say something more about the play.

9. In *Othello* itself, we are offered several possible motives for Iago, but we must make a distinction between those that deserve to be taken seriously and those that do not.

We obviously need not take those motives seriously that are attributed to Iago by others in the course of the action before his plans and actions become manifest. These attributions are a result of Iago's dissimulation, which takes two forms: first, he behaves in such a way that the natural trust which others have in him is confirmed or at least is not undermined; second, Iago generates in others a state of trust that is no longer completely natural, but for the production of which he exploits certain other natural attitudes that people commonly have.

This leaves those motives that need to be taken seriously. Three such motives (or two, depending on the manner of counting) are mentioned in the play, all by Iago himself: (1) he hates Othello for passing him over in promoting Cassio; (2) he hates Othello for supposedly cuckolding him; (3) he is greedy for money. But none of these three motives really explains—or unifies—his action(s) as a whole.

It is true that Iago, with his relentless harangue, practically forces Roderigo to "put money in [his] purse," as he tells him to do eleven times in one dialogue. It is also true that he then proceeds to fleece Roderigo, who does not realize what is happening to him until shortly before the end of the play, at which point Iago finds his death so useful that he brings it about himself. (It is astonishing how psychologically easy it is to give this kind of detached analysis of what happens in a *play*—easy, that is, compared to the difficulties and resistances we experience in analyzing real-life situations.) But this is the *only* place in the play where possessions and wealth are mentioned, and even here they are not really important to Iago. Therefore greed, or one of its relations, is not the passion that dominates Iago, secretly binding his multifarious actions into one whole and merely revealing itself particularly clearly in some passages. If this strand of the action were to be extracted from *Othello* and anonymized, no one but an expert would be able to tell which Shakespeare play it came from. If it is nevertheless significant for the unity of the play, it must be so in a different sense.

The idea that Emilia has deceived Iago with Othello is unlikely to be Iago's prime motive, because he is rather indifferent to her in this respect until she threatens to reveal his hidden activities. The fact that Iago finally stabs Emilia has nothing to do with jealousy—but if not jealousy, what stronger motive could he have for this deed? Or if it is a case of hatred because of marital infidelity, why only in relation to Othello, and not also in relation to Emilia? After all, unity of action does not mean only the unity of everything that really happens, but also that a certain kind of thing *does* happen, unless prevented. If the

agent has a unitary set of motives of a certain kind, one
would expect these motives to express themselves actively
in certain kinds of actions in appropriate circumstances,
provided the actions in question were not impeded by
clear external obstacles. A self-declared admirer of Goya
will cast doubt on his admiration if he does not visit a
Goya exhibition that he could easily visit. That part of his
life whose unity could aptly be characterized by the title
"admirer of Goya" will lose that unity. This could happen not only because something occurs that does not
"fit into the picture" but also because something does *not*
occur that "belongs in the picture," if there is no explanation for its absence. As far as any drama is concerned,
there is really nothing to prevent something happening that "ought to happen" in the sense in which an admirer of Goya "ought," other things being equal, to go
to a Goya exhibition. After all, whatever happens is in
the hands of the dramatist. (Since it is in his hands, the
dramatist may also make mistakes. The insight into this
possibility represents a strong temptation for the inter-
preter, which it may be as useless to resist as is a firm belief in the sanctity of the text.)

If Iago's hatred is due to the preferment of another,
why would this make it necessary for Desdemona, also, to
perish? Why Cassio as well? If Iago is able to persuade
Roderigo to make an attempt on Cassio's life, why not on
that of Othello? After all, Roderigo's supreme goal is to
possess Desdemona, who is connected to Othello and not
to Cassio. Why do all the others have to be dragged into
the affair? And if they have to—for instance because
Othello suffers most when Desdemona dies through his
own fault—why does Iago show no sign of regret for Desdemona? (In this respect compare Iago and Richard III.)

If Iago really believes that he has been passed over un-
fairly, why does he not even begin to defend his actions
by saying so, rather than making his exit without any
comment? Even if we granted that Iago hates Othello for
passing him over, his hatred would clearly go far beyond
what we usually mean by that word; and that would un-
dermine its explanatory power.

Above, I isolated some motives attributed to Iago by
other characters before they saw through his actions.
Bradley suggests that we should not trust one syllable ut-
tered by Iago either, including what he says about himself and in particular about his motives, for example when
he tries to convince Roderigo of his hatred for Othello.[3]
But we do not need Bradley's warning to see that even
when it comes to motives that might be taken seriously,
none that Iago, and Iago alone, puts forward can really
carry the play. On the contrary, what we can observe lends
substance to Bradley's warning, even though it naturally
comes too late to help any of the characters in the play.
In sum: it seems that we can only *speculate* about Iago's
motives.

10. Those who feel obliged to speculate, because they
miss a consistent, clearly recognizable single motive or a
tight bundle of motives in Iago, even though they grant
that the play has a kind of unity, are bound to regard the
lack of an explicit motive as a weakness. And the assertion

---

[3] A. C. Bradley, *Shakespearean Tragedy: Lectures on Hamlet, Othello,
King Lear, Macbeth* (London: Macmillan, 1905), p. 211. As far as the
general point is concerned, in Bradley's view Shakespeare's plays consist above all of "actions in the full sense of the word; not things done
''tween asleep and wake,' but acts or omissions thoroughly expressive
of the doer, —characteristic deeds" (p. 12).

that *Othello*—incidentally the most popular of Shakespeare's plays at all times and particularly in the recent
past—is the most unphilosophical of them all could be
justified by this. For if the motives are so threadbare,
where is the philosophical problem? What is there to
think about in *ethical* terms? What exactly is the morally
relevant unity here? (Note that a conflict such as that of
Oedipus owes half its existence to the fact that Oedipus
has no evil motive. That, too, lends his actions the unity
that matters in the play.) How can we say that Iago is
a *villain* if we learn nothing really believable about his
motives? Because of the effects of his actions on others?
But was the storm that sank the Turkish fleet a villain?
And yet we have no doubt whatsoever that Iago is a villain. On the contrary, to this day he has constantly been
regarded as an *incarnation* of evil. But how can that be?

   Even if the usual judgments about *Othello* are plausible,
they obviously cannot be the whole truth. Maybe, being
half-truths, they even hide the whole truth.

11. Perhaps we should simply say that Iago does what he
does, and leave it at that; he wants to do it because he
wants to do it; he is simply *perverse*. The play is as in-
structive a study as examinations of perversions generally
tend to be. They are fascinating, but they do not plunge
us into the depth of ethical problems, because the moral
weights are too clearly and too artificially distributed. We
are simply shown what other things there are in the world
besides those that exercise us ethically.

   Of course this answer has something going for it. But
even if Iago were merely perverse, the question would
still remain: why does he concern himself with Othello
and Cassio in particular? To put the same question from a

different angle: why does he kill Roderigo and Emilia, rather as if he had no other choice? Why does he not appear gratified when Desdemona's father cannot get over what he regards as the unnatural union of his daughter with an older man who is also black and a foreigner? In short, does Iago not scheme too much in the play to be merely perverse?

These questions should remind us of the obvious fact that, once we have met Iago, what fixes him in our memory forever is not only—or not primarily—his sadism. What makes him remarkable is something else, which is concealed rather than revealed by the label "sadist."

12. What makes Iago remarkable is relegated to the edge of our field of vision if we direct our attention to something that might, from a distance, look like a motive but is not really one. This is how Iago puts it in a conversation with Roderigo:

> We cannot be all masters, nor all masters
> Cannot be truly follow'd. You shall mark
> Many a duteous and knee-crooking knave,
> That, doting on his own obsequious bondage,
> Wears out his time much like his master's ass,
> For nought but provender, and when he's old, cashier'd,
> Whip me such honest knaves: others there are,
> Who, trimm'd in forms, and visages of duty,
> Keep yet their hearts attending on themselves,
> And throwing but shows of service on their lords,
> Do well thrive by 'em, and when they have liv'd in their
>   coats,
> Do themselves homage, those fellows have some soul,
> And such a one do I profess myself, . . . for sir,

It is as sure as you are Roderigo,
Were I the Moor, I would not be Iago:
In following him, I follow but myself.
Heaven is my judge, not I for love and duty,
But seeming so, for my peculiar end.
For when my outward action does demonstrate
The native act, and figure of my heart,
In complement extern, 'tis not long after,
But I will wear my heart upon my sleeve,
For daws to peck at: I am not what I am.

(1.1.43–65)

"Remember not to believe a syllable that Iago utters" was Bradley's advice. But what do we find here to *believe* in any case? That we cannot all be masters? The concept of master is a relational concept. There are no masters if there are no servants. Therefore we cannot *all* be masters, if indeed there are to be any masters at all. We may perhaps abolish the relationship, but that will not make masters of all because once the relationship is abolished, there will no longer be any servants who could have a master. All these are *conceptual* relations, and they are relations that are not, properly speaking, objects of "belief." Rather, those relations exist or they do not, and we can at best *acknowledge* them by using the appropriate words, or by consciously reminding ourselves of what those words mean and how they are used.

This leads us to the next point. Are we to *believe* that anyone is enamored of his servile dependency ("doting on his own obsequious bondage") as Iago understands it? If we follow Iago's line of reasoning, we can hardly believe it, because then we also have to ask ourselves how it would be possible *not* to believe something that, after all,

we see around us everywhere. Isn't it simply a brute observational fact that servants tend to love their servitude?
Not least in the play, in which almost everyone answers
to Iago's verdict. Here the question about Othello's own
condition arises. In fact Othello is answerable to Venice—
and how that appears in the present context is shown by
his last words (which will be briefly examined below). If
even Othello is not only a master, is there anybody at all
who is?

Indeed, Iago does not simply mean that *some* are enamored of their servile dependency while others are not,
but that such is the *rule* among those who are not masters.
We need not believe this, and in any case it is not really
Iago's point. Or can we really believe that Iago might be
diverted from his course by being shown a servant who is
not enamored of his servitude? Iago's point here is the
revelation of a perspective. A perspective, like a concept,
may or may not be adopted, but, again, it is not an object of belief. For Iago, any servants who do not "keep . . .
their hearts attending on themselves" are enamored of
their servile dependency. But the question raised by
Iago's speech is precisely whether those who do "keep . . .
their hearts attending on themselves" can actually be described as servants. Seen in this light, the interesting
thing about Iago's statements is the form in which the
relational nature of master and servant is connected with
the *subjective way of presenting* this relationship.

On the one hand, the tendency of the whole play is to
acknowledge Iago's relationship with Othello (as well as
with Cassio and all the others) as a *plain fact*: Iago is an
ensign and Othello a general and thus his master. On the
other hand, Iago refuses to *acknowledge* the existence of
that same fact: Iago is not Othello's subordinate in reality,

but only in appearance, for *he keeps his own heart to himself*—as if the question whether you are my master, or I am yours, is decided by who keeps his own heart to himself. We cannot answer the question of who is master and who has to serve by looking in people's hearts, *although* it may indeed be the case that servants (tend to) love their masters so that a look into people's hearts may actually reveal who is who. (The relation between Kent and King Lear displays some of these conceptual relations.) Furthermore, if we cannot make a distinction between semblance and being in *this* sense, why should we not all be masters? Admittedly, even if this were the case, this mental phenomenon would change nothing about the social facts. But there is a sense in which the social conditions are not conceivable apart from our acknowledgment of them through attitudes and the like. In fact social conditions are nothing independent of our behavior toward each other. And our behavior in turn is connected with the way we relate to—and what we expect from—ourselves, other people, and the things around us. (That was of course precisely the point of the question about Iago's motive.) Therefore it is not as easy to distinguish between reality and appearance as one might think. On the other hand, it is not surprising that it seems to be easy. One only has to remember how natural it is, for instance, to say that someone has illusions about his situation—or indeed to talk about being enamored of one's own servile dependency. Thus what in one respect is appearance and expressly not reality, in another respect is the form in which the reality must present itself in order to be what it is. In short, Iago plays with ambiguities.

There are only two points in Iago's speech that we could believe in a straightforward sense: his confession of being one of those who keep "their hearts attending on themselves," and the related appeal to self-interest as the motive of his actions or, to put it perhaps better, as the form of his motives.

We can believe Iago's confession, which is basically the reverse side of his view of others, as we believe someone who declares his support for a sports club. This includes the possibility of being deceived about this allegiance. The alleged fan of *this* sports club may in reality have given his heart to another club or to none. Believing a confession includes the possibility of being deceived, and that would seem to require that it be clear *what* exactly Iago confesses to. That, however, is just what is not clear because of the ambiguity with which Iago plays. Is he concerned with the *nature* of the relationship, its *essence*, or its substantial *existence*? What is more, does Iago's idea of the nature of this relationship not expressly exclude the possibility of its having more than the mere appearance of existence? Looked at in this light, the paradox of the confession—one person confessing to another that he is concerned only with himself—appears as a sign of a problem with the content of the confession.

As far as motives are concerned, I have basically covered all the important points, with this exception: If Iago's confession can at all be believed, it is hard to accept that his hatred of Othello is due to the fact that Othello promoted Cassio, rather than him, to be his lieutenant. One can hardly keep one's heart attending on oneself and at the same time hate someone else for not recognizing one's merits. Hatred, after all, is a matter of the heart, and how could another sadden one's own heart if one keeps it attending only on oneself? If there is anyone to whom the phrase "Don't take it personally" is incomprehensible and inapplicable, it is Iago. He is immune to that phrase, not, however, because he takes everything personally but because this formula is already his guiding principle. He does not need to be told. "Don't take it personally" means roughly that this *one* case must be seen in one particular way, implying that other cases must be seen in other ways. Those who take something personally could equally well not take it personally. However, that is precisely out of the question when a person has structured his whole life around devotion to a particular principle. Just as a true pacifist cannot rack his brains as to whether a specific conflict should be resolved by military means, Iago cannot reflect about whether he should take something personally. If he did, he would immediately have betrayed his own principle and, therefore, himself. Because in the play, since Iago is not a person but a concept, as far as such a distinction is possible, he would cease to be Iago if he took anything personally.

This throws light on Harold Bloom's thesis that being slighted by Othello is the "only true motive" of Iago's hatred.[4] Bloom provides the following, apparently plausible, explanation of why Othello passed Iago over: it is precisely because of Iago's nature, which emerges during the play, that Othello did not consider him a suitable replacement for himself on the battlefield, should that become necessary. For Othello, war is a craft (of which, incidentally, he has a masterly command), while for Iago, war is his real element. Othello cannot make Iago his

---

[4] See H. Bloom, *Shakespeare: The Invention of the Human* (New York: Riverhead Books, 1999), p. 434. The next quotation (in which Bloom follows Harold Goddard), ibid. p. 436. I will return to Bloom's interpretation in the Apologia section.

deputy, because a general must be able to distinguish between war and peace, and must strive for the latter. The question, then, is why Othello allows Iago so readily to trap him. Bloom believes that this is because Othello's judgment is well-balanced and reasonable only at the professional level. But in fact the answer is Iago's character. This is revealed when Bloom describes Iago's experience of being passed over as an "ontological shock . . . the trauma that truly creates Iago, no mere wicked Ensign but rather a genius of evil who has engendered himself from a great Fall."

This explanation casts doubt on its own starting point. If being passed over is really an ontological shock, how can the play reveal what is said to be Iago's already existing nature? (The devil is a fallen angel. *Must* such an angel be in some way evil before the fall? Can he, being an angel? Is the omnipotence of the Lord not shown more conclusively by the fact that there is nothing about the angel that argues in advance for his fall, no compulsion of any kind that the Lord would have to obey—and that would make his actions more intelligible to us?) Furthermore, if the true Iago is created by being passed over, he cannot be the cause of being passed over. This forces Bloom to describe the pretransfigured Iago as having no conscience. But the text contains no evidence of this. We see how serious the situation can become if a clear and strong motive that would guarantee the unity of the action is missing.

The problem is not that the spectator or reader is not allowed to add anything to the text in order to generate a coherence and completeness that are not there. There is a sense in which it is not even possible to refrain from going beyond the text. For example, it is not insignificant that

Othello is said to be a Moor. But just how dark is his skin, and how light is Desdemona's? And how long are Iago's fingernails? Othello's and Desdemona's skin must be some shade, and Iago's fingernails some length (if he has any, and the play does not tell us that he has none . . .). But how could we stage the play if we relied only on what is said in the text? Would the spectator not have the right to wonder what it would mean if Iago's fingernails were a foot in length—what it would mean for the play or its performance, of course? In this sense, surely, nobody has ever advocated the view that nothing should be read into a text that is not expressly stated in it. (The fact that there can be more than one justifiable interpretation makes it more difficult to follow this maxim, but not impossible.) The point is, rather, that nothing should be read into a text that could influence the interpretation of its more significant elements. But that is exactly what needs to happen if we follow Bloom's proposition.

However, there seems to be one passage actually in the play that confirms Iago's assertion that he is driven by self-interest. It is Emilia's remark to Desdemona about men, which one cannot help reading as a verdict on her marriage to Iago:

> 'Tis not a year or two shows us a man:
> They are all but stomachs, and we all but food;
> They eat us hungerly, and when they are full,
> They belch us out.
>
> (3.4.100–103)

But is Emilia's remark really as strong an endorsement of Iago's statement as it initially might seem to be? If one were to understand it that way, the difference between the two individuals could not be so fundamental that what was apparently the same statement meant two completely different things when said by the one and by the other. In that case Iago would lose the quality of being more different from the other actors than they are from each other. His absolute otherness would be forfeited. Basically, he would be just like Emilia, only at the other end of the spectrum that determines both. The starting point of the whole story, however, is precisely that he is not at all like Emilia but totally exceptional.

13. This brings us back to Iago's most famous line. He says, "I am not what I am" and not "I am not what I seem to be." Is this a concentrated poetic statement that the spectator can construe as he likes? "I am not what I seem to be, but I am also what I seem to be, albeit in a different way from being what I do not seem to be"? Is Shakespeare teaching us, as it were in passing, that appearance is essential for being, that the being of a man is nothing other than what he is *seen* to feel, think, do, and refrain from doing? To say, then, in an emphatic way that he *appears* to be such and such, although he *really* is not, is to say that some other person has only a restricted or partial view of him, that is, does not see everything that could in principle be seen. (This is in contrast to the position we occupy as spectators of that play and thus witnesses of Iago's soliloquies. By definition, we do see and hear all there is to see and hear.)

This interpretation would solve the mystery only if everything that there was to be seen revealed a motive that made Iago's actions sufficiently understandable. If what he claims to be his motive, although it is not, emerged, for example, from his soliloquies; if *we*, at least, the spectators of the play, could see it; if it were visible in principle—then his actions, and therefore he himself, would explicitly be not what they seem. But he has no such motive; he has only pseudomotives.

1.3. IAGO'S MODE OF BEING AND THE IDEA OF A PANOPTICON

14. Instead of continuing to search for an answer to the question of motive, it is perhaps time to take a different route. Naturally, we must avoid ending up once more by simply noting Iago's perversity. Actually, we are left with only one option: that of considering the fact that a plausible motive is missing as the point of the whole story.[5] To be accurate, in this case it is not actually *missing*, because something that is not *meant* to exist is not missing if it does not exist. With the absence of a consistent motive emerging as the real point of the story, perversity, too, appears in a new light.

The philosophically interesting sense in which Iago's motive is missing is acknowledged in Coleridge's well-

---

[5] Stephen Greenblatt, *Will in the World: How Shakespeare Became Shakespeare* (New York: Norton, 2004), talks about the opacity of *Othello* caused by the "excision of motive" and contrasts this with the opacity of *Macbeth*. But the opacity persists only as long as one approaches the play with a specific expectation. Macbeth is a schemer and not an Iago, but both can be seen through. If something is different from something else on the one hand and alike on the other, we may of course find it difficult to recognize what we are up against (at a particular moment). This may easily evoke an impression of opacity. Incidentally, what I have said about Macbeth also holds for Richard III. But in his case in particular the difference from Iago is clearly recognizable. Richard III clearly shows us a continuous motive. (On the schemer, see below.)

known image of Iago's activities as the "motive-hunting of a motiveless malignity": Iago is indeed constantly hunting for a motive because no motive really moves him in the way in which motives move normal people. This, in turn, is the case because no motive is really important to him. However, since in Iago's case one also cannot, for the reasons stated above, say that a motive is really missing, the image of "motive-hunting" is inappropriate insofar as it suggests that Iago is concerned to have one. On Coleridge's reading one might say that clutching at a motive (any motive?) would be his real motive. Having a motive matters to Iago, however, only insofar as it enables him to do what he has really set his heart on, and that is not simply sadism or malice, as will be shown. This makes his quest for a motive itself appear as a motive. The consequences for the spectator or reader can be warded off through a recognition of the paradoxes in Coleridge's image.

Shakespeare, to be sure, teaches us a further lesson about the connections between appearance and reality in *Othello*: we should trust what we are offered by the play, and we should judge our ideas by what happens onstage, rather than the other way round. But that is only a secondary aspect of the effect the play is supposed to have on us. What is more important is that this attitude to the play, far from making our problem disappear, allows us to see it quite clearly for the first time.

The problem has two dimensions.

15. The first dimension takes us back to Iago's great line "I am not what I am." *What*, then, is a man who does all kinds of things, not least risking his own life, without a real motive?

Recall Johnson's dictum that "nothing is essential to the fable but unity of action." Without unity of action there is no plot, and without a motive there is no unity of action. We have no continuous motive that would make *Othello* as a whole intelligible, but we do have a plot. It is the plot I summarized earlier. At the same time, we have no plot, in another sense, because in that summary I was unable to mention something essential to plot: the motive. Where something essential is missing, there is a conceptual or logical gap. A man who lacks a wife may lack something actual; a husband who lacks a wife lacks something conceptual. This lack, for him, carries such weight that he is not what he is. Where there is a conceptual gap, we are faced with something illogical. In Iago's "I am not what I am" the illogical as such is articulated at one of the most conspicuous points in the drama. Seen in conceptual terms, a man who acts deliberately without a motive—and there can be little doubt either about the deliberateness of Iago's actions or about the absence of a clearly recognizable motive behind them—is something that is not what it is: an impossibility.

The spectator's, or reader's, awareness of this fact could be said to express itself in a wrongheaded interpretation of the play in exclusively psychopathological terms, which denies its ethical—or, more generally, philosophical—content. It is wrongheaded because the pathological has no independent existence of its own, since it is determined by its relation to the nonpathological, the healthy. At the same time a pathological case is not simply one among many. A frog with three legs is still a frog, simply not a frog like all the others. Viewed in this way, Iago is a teratological phenomenon, a monstrous being.

16. This immediately draws our attention to the second dimension. The play does not simply unfold a traditional story—of the kind that begins with such and such things happening for such and such reasons, before other outcomes intervene, replacing or running parallel to the intended ones, and forcing the actor to change his original plan or to modify his original intentions, while preserving certain aims, passions, and so forth, as the basic motive. Naturally, that is the *form* of (a great deal of) drama. But the more willing we are to accept the fact that in our story such a motive is poorly developed, the easier it will be for us to understand the traditional form of this story as a disguise for something else: the play really presents a panopticon.[6] (The discussion of self-interest as a *form* of motive—see section 9 above—already points in this direction.)

To put it more precisely: In *Othello* we are shown, largely by way of a traditional dramatic process, a series of *images* that are interconnected through their similarity and thus form a whole. These images are distinct enough to allow a succession of other images to be seamlessly attached to them, extending them in different directions. The whole array gives a kind of overview of the concept in question by exhibiting in an ordered way the manifold different visible forms the phenomena falling under the concept can take. Just as a field guide to plants could manage with

---

[6] My version of a panopticon is related to Goethe's idea of "elective affinities" and Wittgenstein's concept of family resemblance. Both are methods of "perspicuous representation," as stated in section 122 of the *Philosophical Investigations*, trans. G.E.M. Anscombe (New York: Macmillan, 1955) (see also sections 65ff.), or part of a morphology, as imagined by Goethe.

a series of pictures alone, without any text, gradually allowing the reader to form the concepts of "primrose," "fern," "daffodil," and so on, so *Othello*, through its successive scenes, defines what one might call the "concept of Iago." But given that this is a concept of something pathological, the totality of the scenes can be viewed as presenting a systemically organized visible display of curious, deviant, and otherwise noteworthy phenomena; a display of this kind will be called a "panopticon."

17. Of course, there is a certain tension between the idea of a panopticon and that of a dramatic action. Indeed, there must be tension, if dramatic action is marked by a kind of sequential necessity, with this leading to that, that following from this, and all tied together by a continuous motive, a passion, a character trait, or the like. What seems to be lost if we consider the play as a panopticon of scenes is precisely the the sense of inexorable necessity.

To put it differently, if *Othello* really is a panopticon, why does Shakespeare not give it the corresponding dramatic form right from the outset? Why does he not simply write a series of separate scenes, as Brecht does, for example, in *The Private Life of the Master Race*? Bearing in mind the lack of sequential unity in some medieval and early modern drama, we can hardly assume that Shakespeare did not know that dramatic form. What are the implications of this for the internal form—that is, the structure—of the play?

The problem of necessity in the sequence of events is addressed in the play itself, when Iago says,

> The Moor already changes with my poison:
> Dangerous conceits are in their nature poisons,

> Which at the first are scarce found to distaste,
> But with a little act upon the blood
> Burn like the mines of sulphur.
>
>   (3.3.330–34)

The metaphor naturally corresponds to the customary image: as many poisons take effect gradually, so in the play one thing evolves from another. This would seem to be a clear image of a (kind of) necessity. But on closer inspection the supposed clarity of the image vanishes.

Nothing is inherently or in itself a poison. To call something a "poison" is to speak relationally, that is, to describe its effects on something else. We do sometimes say that something is "a poison" *simpliciter*, but when we do that, we are always, as it were, tacitly referring to a set of parameters that are well known to those with whom we are speaking. These sets of parameters may vary from case to case. In any case, statements like "This is poisonous" are often warnings, not information. If, then, as we saw earlier with the concept of a lord, the concept of poison is a relational concept, the basic unit, so to speak, is the whole comprising the dangerous idea, the person on whom it has such and such an effect, and finally the effect itself. One might object that the last point is valid only if everything runs its normal course. It is true that the effect of a poison may perhaps be postponed or even canceled by means of an antidote, but this does not mean that we are overhasty or inaccurate if we say without further qualification that something is poisonous, rather than spelling out, more correctly, that it is poisonous *if* no antidote is administered, or if the recipient does not die of something else beforehand. It is correct to say that

if one player passes the ball too vigorously, the other will
not be able to get control of it. It is no more correct to
say that the second player will not get control of the ball
unless it inexplicably stops in its tracks or the second
player suddenly finds himself able to react three times as
fast as he usually can; this is true despite the fact that
it is *imaginable* that the ball might suddenly stop or the
second player suddenly put on an unprecedented burst
of speed. To say that the ball was passed too vigorously
means that it was passed too fast for a normal player
(under normal circumstances) to get it. That something
is poisonous *means* that (usually) it has such and such an
effect on the normal human constitution. It is the same
in drama. Naturally, it is possible to imagine events that
would throw a spanner in Iago's plans. Let us imagine
that in the middle of the play a meteorite destroyed the
whole of Cyprus, just as the storm at the beginning of
the play destroys the whole of the Turkish fleet. Only
because the Turkish fleet was destroyed did Othello
have the time and, as it were, the leisure to be entangled
in Iago's machinations. Did Shakespeare make a mistake
when he conjured up the storm but said nothing about
this possible meteorite, and what would have happened if
it had struck?

The strangeness and absurdity of the question throws
light on the nature of drama: it is a kind of *logic*. By means
of a single "event" it shows us the *essence* of a thing. Since
it is a kind of event, it is also up to us whether we follow it
like a football match, because it is no less exciting, or
whether we devote a different kind of attention to it by
taking Montaigne's advice "to pick out and put to use
what happens before our eyes, and to judge it keenly

enough to make it an example."[7] And should we not find this even easier when we contemplate something that—unlike life itself, of which Montaigne speaks—was expressly made to be seen by the human eye?

As far as our topic is concerned, the following remark in chapter 13 of Machiavelli's *The Prince* is of interest: "But men have so little judgement and foresight that they initiate policies that seem attractive, without noticing any poison that is concealed, as I said earlier, when referring to consumptive fevers. Therefore, a ruler who does not recognise evils in the very early stages cannot be considered wise; this ability is given only to few."[8] What is the nature of the wisdom in question?

Let us assume that a person has an illness that normally manifests itself little by little. What if for once it does *not* manifest itself, for example because the patient made a speedy spontaneous recovery? In this case we do not simply say that he was not *really* ill but only *seemed* to be. On the other hand, neither do we say that a person suffering from tuberculosis will *probably* undergo a certain process. We *know* that tuberculosis develops in such and such a way. To be more accurate, we should say: it is part of our concept of tuberculosis that it takes such and such a

---

[7] M. de Montaigne, "Of Experience," in *Essais* (Paris: Langelier, 1580–1587), quoted from *The Complete Essays of Montaigne*, trans. Donald M. Frame (Stanford, CA: Stanford University Press, 1965), p. 828.

[8] Niccolò Machiavelli, *The Prince*, ed. Quentin Skinner and Russell Price (Cambridge: Cambridge University Press, 2007), p. 50f. (The context of this remark is an inquiry into "Auxiliaries, mixed troops and native troops." But the remark quoted draws a more general lesson. See also my comments in section 33.)

course. Two factors must be considered here. First, we
say that tuberculosis takes such and such a course because
that is what generally happens and because we have experienced it that way. In that sense the wisdom Machiavelli demands of the prince is the wisdom of the man of
experience. But experience alone is not enough to generate a concept. It is slightly off the mark to say that
we have the concept of tuberculosis because "we have
experienced" tuberculosis; experiences, after all, can be
"processed" in many different ways. Second, therefore,
what might be called an element of arbitrariness is always present in any diagnosis. It is we who *determine* that
something that takes such and such a course should be
regarded as tuberculosis, and called by that name, while
anything that does not take that course—as can be more
or less accurately determined—simply is not tuberculosis
and should not bear this name. Seen in this light, the
prince's wisdom is a conceptual wisdom, although naturally the concept would not need to be explicitly formulated and defined by the prince himself. Thus the prince
may determine that something is a danger to the state by
acting in a certain way, for instance by suppressing it or
punishing those involved in it, without explicitly calling it
"a danger to the state."

The connection between the two factors, which I have
separated for the purposes of analysis only, is provided by
the wisdom of a prince who is able to assess the nature of
things accurately at an early point and who will therefore
recognize in good time what he is up against. For if the
tendency to take such and such a course is part of the
nature, or concept, of tuberculosis and not just one of its
empirical consequences, then the man with the correct
conceptual grasp of the phenomena will not (normally) be

surprised by later developments. Not only is the frequency with which he can be surprised in inverse proportion to the frequency with which things follow the exact course implied in the concept, but if he is truly wise he will never be surprised, since his understanding of this relationship—of what is normal and what is deviant but possible—is part of his understanding of the things themselves. For he expects only what is in the nature of things, and if it is in their nature to be unpredictable in a certain respect, he will expect nothing specific in that respect. Where there is no expectation, there is no surprise, because we are surprised when something does not happen as expected.

Let us return to Othello. His receptivity to Iago's whispers tells us from the outset that dangerous thoughts affect him like poison. That poison, however, does not simply transform him into a completely different person. Rather, something for which he already has a predisposition erupts, unfolds, and becomes manifest, that is, visible to everybody, not least to Othello himself. Those who claim that Iago undergoes an ontological transformation can hardly find it within the play and will have to look for it outside. The same applies to Othello.

The poison that Iago administers to Othello, then, is a poison because Othello is receptive to it. Othello's receptivity means, in the general sense of Iago's speech quoted above, that in his case we find it difficult to identify a self that is not absorbed in others, just as in the case of Iago we hesitate to talk about an individuated self at all, because for him no true *other* self exists with which he could be contrasted. We do not know what other selves, in his own eyes, Iago could be confronting. Just as Othello loves Desdemona, so he trusts Iago, and he is fully absorbed by both (as he was before, and to some extent still is, by his office).[9] This weakness of Othello in comparison to Iago, which constantly astounds the spectator, is conceptually determined: Othello is the counterpart of Iago. What is too strong in Iago is too weak in Othello. What Iago denies is the substance of Othello. For Iago a good name is nothing, while Othello does "all in honour" (5.2.296) Compare this to Cassio— who resembles Othello more in his speeches than in his deeds, as is revealed not least in his relationship with his "friend" Bianca. If Iago represents a problem, so does Othello, for both raise the same issue. If we understand the play primarily as a story about the devastating effect of jealousy, that of "all the diseases of the mind . . . which the most things serve to feed and the fewest things to remedy,"[10] we may well be annoyed by the speed, indeed the alacrity, with which Othello succumbs to Iago's whispers. In that case the story would not profit us very much. But if we turn the examination around, things will look rather different. It will then become clear that

[9] See Tzachi Zamir's interpretation of Othello in *Double Vision: Moral Philosophy and Shakespearean Drama* (Princeton: Princeton University Press, 2007), pp. 151–67.

[10] Montaigne, "Upon Some Verses of Virgil," in *Essais*, p. 658. Montaigne articulates an important and profound idea, but merely because it is profound and important it need not be the main idea of *Othello*. If it were the main idea, the ease with which Othello succumbs to that illness would appear to be a downright trivialization. Therefore it is advisable to understand Montaigne's remark differently from what it seems at first sight to suggest. In what follows, I will show that the devastating effect of jealousy is not like the destruction of a shed struck by lightning, but something more "inward." The method, if it can be so described, is the examination of an illness of the human mind.

what makes jealousy the most devastating illness of the human mind is that ultimately it destroys not only the mind itself but things that originally had nothing to do with it.

Let us consider, for example, the difference between Othello and Iago in terms of their respective development. We can say that Othello undergoes a certain development, while Iago does not. But what a pathetic development it is. Othello simply keels over. (And later he keels over again, just as promptly, in the opposite direction.) But that is exactly the point. Othello remains the same in that he is always *primarily* defined by his relations with others. The *kind* or *direction* of these relations may change, but his relation-dependence remains the same. Othello is as dependent as Iago is self-reliant. He even leaves Cassio to woo Desdemona on his behalf, so that in this domain, too, there is nothing to counteract the impression of dependence he makes. In this light the frequently raised question whether he has actually consummated his marriage to Desdemona assumes a special significance. If he has not, his marriage looks even more like a purely social relationship—except that if he lacked independence completely, he would be unable even to enter into such a relationship. (Where could one demonstrate more directly that one "keeps one's heart attending on oneself" than in a pretended intimate relationship?) Nor is the ease and speed of Othello's transformation a problem; it is a sign for the nature of the process involved. It is not a dogged, steady change, no difficult birth, but a quick bound or a kind of slide into a different mode of existence, which is connected to the previous one and, as will be seen in his downfall, dependent on it. Othello's movements resemble those of a metronome, which one can understand only if one sees them as segments of a unitary motion around *one* point. In contrast, Iago remains all the time what he is, or, more accurately, what he believes he is. In the course of the play we are shown what he stands for, as he smoothly moves from one sphere of life to the next. In this respect, Iago's movements resemble those of an oil slick on the surface of the sea: the oil easily changes its form depending on how the waves and the winds change, but it never mixes with the water.

The degree of continuity, or the extent of the homogeneity of the whole, is also an effect of the play's form, and in this instance a great deal of homogeneity would be lost if the play consisted simply of a more or less loose sequence of scenes. In fact it is so homogeneous that the "effect" of Iago's poison appears, as it were, as a conceptual matter rather than a factual process (see above). And just as we are reminded by it of Machiavelli's remark about the wise statesman, or of Montaigne's aperçu about jealousy, we could easily think of Wittgenstein's remark "Pride is like an infection, a fever. It isn't located like a sore thumb. The fever permeates the whole body. So pride too."[11] If pride permeates the whole (moral) body of the person, it must also be found, to a certain extent, in

---

[11] This remark is reported by O. K. Bouwsma, *Wittgenstein: Conversations 1949–1951*, ed. and introd. J. L. Craft and R. E. Hustwit (Indianapolis: Hackett, 1986), pp. 4–5. On the speed of Othello's transformation, see also Stanley Cavell, "Othello and the Stake of the Other," in *Disowning Knowledge in Seven Plays of Shakespeare*, updated ed. (Cambridge: Cambridge University Press, 2003), pp. 125–42, particularly p. 128. According to Cavell, pp. 129–31, it is wrong to ask why Othello believes Iago, because it is unimaginable that he should believe Iago and not Desdemona. Rather, Iago offers Othello an opportunity "to believe something, something to oppose to something

each part of the body. If we find it in one part, we may easily believe that we have located it and, as it were, pinned it down, and that therefore we know where to start getting rid of it. That this is not possible if pride permeates the *whole* body is easily overlooked. If pride permeates the whole body, it must be present in all parts of the body, and therefore it would seem natural to search the parts for the cause of the disease. In countless cases it is natural, and indeed right, to do so. But if we encounter the cause of the disease in one part of the body, we still cannot be sure of having really localized it. We must also be certain that it is not like a fever that permeates the whole body. Without this certainty, there will be a mismatch between the idea or the concept that we have formed of it and the method of getting rid of it. If we approach it from the image or concept of a fever (or of a poisoned body), we are less likely to make that mistake. Applied to the play, this image means seeing all the individual scenes as symptoms of the same thing. The scenes themselves may be different from each other, just as the temperature of a person with a fever need not be the same in all parts of his body. (We measure the temperature of a person's *body* in *specific* places.)

To return to a comparison we have already made, just as in a field guide each picture of a fungus is designed not only to show the particular fungus in question, but also to

---

else he knows." A model of this interpretation is supplied by Hermione's words to Leontes (in *The Winter's Tale*, 3.2.31–34):

> You, my lord, best know
> Who least will seem to do so, my past life
> Hath been as continent, as chaste, as true,
> As I am now unhappy.

make a contribution to explaining the concept of fungus in general, so each scene of the play contributes to the definition of the *concept* of Iago. However, just as the image of one fungus is only one of many that make up the definition, so each individual scene has a significance only in the context of the play. This idea can be derived from what we know about other plays, and to that extent it is justifiable.

Here the real significance of Iago's deception of Roderigo, as part of the play, also becomes clear. Seen in traditional terms, it has no essential significance. It simply appears as an expression of avarice. But since avarice is obviously not one of Iago's salient features, its appearance would not only mystify but actually distract us from his essential motive—if there is one. Seen in the new light, however, the deception is an integral part of the whole. It demonstrates something about Iago that has really nothing to do with avarice but that serves as a further example of his attitude to others. The deception is one self-contained image from a series of images that make Iago's character visible.

In this respect, then, the ordering of the scenes in *Othello* is quasi-spatial: everything stands side by side with everything else, as in a panopticon. Anything that is chronologically arranged in relation to Iago (and, with some modifications, to Othello) belongs neither to the character nor to the concept exemplified by the character, but to the *form* of the play.

Nevertheless, even though it is possible to arrange scenes in a panopticon in different ways, just as it is possible to arrange the illustrations of plants in a field guide according to different points of view, this does not mean that no necessity of any kind can be found in a panopticon. In some arrangements the internal coherence of what is represented is more visible than in others. In a series of portraits, for example, the order in which the pictures follow each other cannot be ignored if the series is to reveal the family relationship of the sitters. In the ideal case, everything seems all of a piece, as in a morphing sequence: we may begin with the portrait of a person, say, the head of the government, and change this seamlessly step-by-step until we have a different face before us, say, that of the leader of the opposition. The process is not an arbitrary one. For example, it is not possible simply to juxtapose the beginning and the end of the series right at the outset; if one were to do this, one would run the risk of failing to reveal the similarity between the end points. Although there can be several—to be precise, an infinity of—series, this does not mean that any one arrangement for which we may opt will exemplify the same thing or bring out the same similarity equally well. Once we have decided to place this or that image at the head of the series, we may place countless other things beside it, but there are some we must avoid, if we do not want to obscure their inner coherence. If one starts with *this*, one cannot continue with whatever happens to come to mind.

18. In light of what I have said above, two further images immediately fall into place. The first concerns the way Iago exits at the end of the play.

> Demand me nothing, what you know, you know,
> From this time forth I never will speak word.
>
> (5.2.304–5)

"What you know, you know"—is this to be read in the
sense in which one might say that one is as fat as one is,
or that one's hair is the color it is? Hardly. "What you
know, you know" means: What you know is all there is to
know. There is no motive (as in the case of Lady Macbeth);
there is no anguish (as in the case of Richard III); there
is nothing behind that which is known. What is visible
speaks for itself, and that is all there is. As soon as it is clear
that the game is up, Iago falls silent. He does not defend
himself; he does not repent; he does not pray; he does not
show any reaction to the threat of torture. Although to
some extent he surrenders, he does so by withdrawing as
far as he can short of taking his own life. He certainly does
not undergo any moral awakening or purification, which
would allow him to accept and be reconciled to his fate.
(In retrospect this also marks the words he used a little
earlier to silence Emilia, which might be interpreted as a
faint sign of his acceptance of morality.) What else could
he do, once the time for "shows of service on . . . lords"
has passed and since in any case he "keeps his heart attending" only on himself? For Iago, nobody exists apart
from himself. Against whom, then, *could* he defend himself? Even assuming that he did something that induced
others to forgive him or at least to consider seeking some
extenuating circumstances on his behalf, what could that
mean to a character who has no room whatsoever in his
heart for others? And what action could make Othello a
more obvious counterpart of Iago than his suicide? More-
over, a suicide introduced by Othello's recollection of
his services to the republic and a brief account of how

> in Aleppo once,
> Where a malignant and a turban'd Turk

Beat a Venetian, and traduc'd the state,
[He] took by the throat the circumsized dog,
And smote him thus.

$$(5.2.353–57)$$

What exits! How different and at the same time how alike!

The second point that might be taken to support a reading of the play as a panopticon, and that at the same time leads us back to the teratoid nature of Iago, is that in centuries past his mere appearance onstage was often accompanied by hissing from the audience and by exclamations to Othello, Cassio, and others enjoining them to beware of him. Even if this was to some extent a result, or a part, of a particular tradition of performance, there is no doubt that Johnson is correct when he writes, "[T]he character of Iago is so conducted that he is from the first scene to the last hated and despised."[12] This indicates the role attributed to Iago's actions from the very beginning (in the eyes of the spectators, who of course make the play a play). The hissing started even before he tied the next knot in the net in which both he and Othello were in the end hopelessly to ensnarl themselves. There is therefore a sense in which his actions themselves cannot really be the decisive factor in explaining this reaction of the audience. Whatever he may do, we sense very early what he is up to.

---

[12] Johnson, *Plays of William Shakespeare*, p. 466. This is an extremely noteworthy sentence in a text that places such emphasis on the "unity of action." It is also of interest insofar as *Othello* is a drama of disclosure, in which all that matters lies open all the time. The two reflections combine in the idea of a panopticon: we come to see the nature of a thing only gradually, but not because something that has been concealed is suddenly brought to light.

At the same time this can be revealed only by what he actually does. How else could it be? But Iago's being is defined less by the sequence of his actions as such than by something else, of which that sequence is only a specimen. The actual event could have been replaced by something—but not just anything—else. We could almost say that watching Iago we have the *same* feeling, no matter what he does. But this sameness is neither located beyond the sequence of events nor hidden within it or its parts. We sense it before we see or recognize it, not by intuiting in the events something that is not visible, but by construing the events as part of a sequence even before the sequence really unfolds. Thus Iago undergoes no real development, as does, for example, Roderigo. Indeed he does not even experience a change, as does Othello, not to mention other dramatic characters such as Oedipus, Faust, or Brecht's Señora Carrar.

Finally, if we take away from Iago his hatred, are we left without an Iago? When the curtain has fallen and the book has been closed, does Iago stand before us (primarily) as a formidable hater? Is what he stands for not something completely different? Something that is connected with his *actions as such* and more or less detached from the *reasons* for those actions?

19. What, however, is the *same thing* that manifests itself in all of Iago's actions? In other words, what concept of him is indicated by this dramatic panopticon? Here I return to the reflection that the vagueness of Iago's motives should be regarded not as a weakness of the play, but as the very point of it.

If the play presents Iago as the very paradigm of something, then this paradigm includes the relative unimportance of a motive. If, however, the motive disappears in the background, what remains, apart from Iago's method of operating? If this method consists in nothing but what the sequence or series of his actions manifests, then the absence of a clear specification of Iago's motive proves to be an essential point! Iago's method of operating itself is the main issue. For any motive that could explain Iago's actions as a whole would shift the weight of the examination away from his method toward what drives him, say, for example, the passion of jealousy or hatred. But how can a method be represented without the display of an actual operation of it? Since a real operation is essentially determined by a motive, nothing is better suited to be a model of the method of operating itself than a *pathological case* of action, that is, an action without a clear motive. Such a case is Iago. The play reveals a double unity. As in a panopticon, we are shown a number of images that reflect the essence of a matter through their internal relations. However, these images are not merely lined up to exhibit a particular kind of unity. They are directly integrated by the form of the play. The danger of a traditional essentialist interpretation is averted through the absence of a motive in the main character.

I will try to phrase the same thing in a way that might less readily invite the misunderstanding that the motive plays *no part at all*. What I wish to claim can best be expressed as a disjunction: *Either* motives do not play the part they normally play in action, and that part is played by Iago's method of operating—his way of dealing with others. *Or* the usual human motives play the role they usually play in human life, but for Iago a certain way of dealing with people has become an all-consuming passion; in some sense his *real* motive is his method. It is as if we said about a gambler either that he is not concerned about the end or goal of gambling, or that for him gambling has become its own purpose. The gambler gambles for the sake of gambling, even at the risk of his own destruction. What is pathological here is not only, if at all, his willingness to act at the risk of his own destruction, but rather the compulsiveness of his need to gamble. Even a gambler who is usually successful is, if he is an addict, a pathological case. It is the operation as such that fascinates and also dooms Iago. His destruction without catharsis represents in a temporal form what I expressed above in a timeless way by saying that Iago is a teratological phenomenon, a monster inexorably fated to destroy himself.

This in turn implies that replacing destructive, self-regarding motives with constructive, altruistic ones would not alter anything fundamental about the evaluation of the procedure Iago follows. We see this when we remind ourselves that our image of Iago is not above all else that of a passionate hater. The passion that constitutes Iago, as far as it is a passion, is of a different kind.

20. To continue the discussion of Iago as a teratological phenomenon, a logically self-destructive being: of course it is not the case that we could have no idea of the concept of Iago if Shakespeare had not written his play. It is rather the reverse: we understand this play, as far as we do understand it, because we are familiar with the sort of thing that happens in it, or, more precisely, because we are familiar with the human material on which Shakespeare draws. As in the case of Iago, a germ of what comes to fruition in *Othello* is contained in everybody who under-

stands the play, in accordance with the old insight that like is recognized only by like.

Nevertheless, a certain vagueness prevails, because it is not quite clear how close what Shakespeare presents really is to what we already know from everyday life, or to what extent what makes something that is implicit explicit is also different from what it makes explicit.[13] In any case Shakespeare's play is neither a simple photographic picture of anything familiar nor anything one might compose by simply putting together familiar elements in a novel way. It is something distinctive. To that extent *Othello* introduces us to more than just the possibility of

[13] Hegel believes that in "the exposition of fully developed human characters and personality," Shakespeare stands "at an almost unapproachable height" (*Ästhetik*, ed. F. Bassenge, 2nd ed. [Berlin: Aufbau, 1984], 2:577. English quotation from *Hegel and Tragedy*, ed. and introd. Anne and Henry Paolucci [New York: Harper & Row, 1962], p. 85). In contrast, Wittgenstein notes: "It is *not* as if S[hakespeare] were good at portraying human types & in so far *true*. He is *not* true to nature. But he has such a supple hand & such a peculiar *brush stroke* that every one of his characters looks *significant*, worth seeing" (*Wittgensteins Nachlaß: The Bergen Electronic Edition* [Oxford: Oxford University Press, 2000], item 173, p. 35r, v, 36r.). If, on hearing the phrase "fully developed human characters," we think of characters as we know them from life, for Hegel Shakespeare is "almost unapproachable" because of his truthfulness. Wittgenstein, in Ms 126b, p. 61r, v, notes: "One could say that Shakespeare shows the dance of human passions. Therefore he must remain objective, otherwise he would not show the dance of human passions—but rather talk about it. But he shows them in the dance, not in a naturalistic fashion. (I got this idea from Paul Engelmann.)" Unlike the idea of the supple hand, Engelmann's idea indeed looks like a link between the judgment of Hegel and the first thought of Wittgenstein, which otherwise appear as total opposites. And both that judgment and this idea force themselves on us in relation to *Othello* in the shape of the impression of a panopticon and in the form of the idea of the unified and everywhere recognizable character of Iago. (See my remarks about motivation,

giving a familiar thing a new name. We are introduced to
something new, although it has no real, independent
existence of its own. Therefore, one might expect it to be
merely an old thing in a new perspective, which shows us
the true nature of that thing. It shows it to us by leading
us to its limits.

21. This should have made clear that the "concept of
Iago" is not simply a different term for "scheming," just
as Iago himself is not simply a schemer. For schemers, of
the kind that interest us, are not simply humans who happen at some time to engage in some scheming, but people
whose very nature it is to be constantly scheming.

   If we call someone a schemer, we are not usually being
morally neutral. In fact it is one of the worst things we
can say.

   This is not without a certain irony because, since being
a schemer is one of the worst things a human being can
be, accusing someone else of scheming is eminently suited
to be itself part of a scheme. For this reason accusing
someone else of scheming can be a proleptic defense
against the accusation of being a schemer oneself, just

---

particularly about the third supposed motive, in section 9 above.) My
view is also indebted to Engelmann's idea. It allows, among other
things, what James Shapiro calls the "platitude that a dramatist can
best be understood in relation to his time" to be reconciled with, e.g.,
Ben Jonson's view that Shakespeare belongs "not to one time but all
times," which is a similar platitude. See Shapiro, *1599: A Year in the
Life of William Shakespeare* (London: Faber and Faber, 2005), pp. xvif.,
where the quotation from Jonson is also referred to. But where two
platitudes seem to clash, a reconciliation is obviously needed. If
Shakespeare is (or was?) not *true* in Engelmann-Wittgenstein's sense,
both platitudes say too little to be simply either accepted or rejected.
This is where the possibility of reconciling them rests.

as accusing somebody of being a schemer can be part of a scheme. In fact, *announcing* the truth I have just formulated—that accusing someone else of being a schemer can itself be part of a scheme—can in turn form part of a kind of metascheme. And so on. (This in itself is not a form of skepticism, which does not appear until one adds the hypothesis that one cannot know in *any* case what the thing in question is.)

22. What exactly is so bad about the accusation of scheming? That it is aimed at damaging or even destroying a person's good reputation. In the context of the play there is a tendency to identify a person's good reputation with his moral standing as such. Cassio's speech is a particularly vivid expression of this tendency. His good reputation is what Cassio believes to be the immortal part of himself; what remains if this is lost is the animal part (see 2.3.254–56).

At least for Cassio—and in a certain sense for those who see him, all things considered, as a noble character—the moral substance of a person consists (among other things) of his good reputation. Since this substance is what constitutes him as a human being rather than an animal, it is *he* who will be destroyed if his reputation is destroyed. If he survived the destruction of his reputation, his life would no longer be one that he would call "human." He might still live *among* human beings, but rather like a dog, not *with* them as a fellow human. To Cassio, his humanity is not something internal that he owns alone and exclusively. Nor is it simply a property attached to him. We do not have a good reputation in the same way as we have a body of a certain size. A good reputation is something one has among *other* people; it is not so much a property as a relation. To use a well-known formula, the nature of a human being is not something intrinsic to him but rather a network of relations, particularly relations involving esteem and recognition, appreciation, respect, and the like—in short, a good reputation. For Cassio, his good name is a matter of life and death. (Thus suicide as a reaction to the—supposed—loss of honor does not seem purely conventional. At best it is conventional in a derivative sense; it has its origins in the convention of seeing honor as the substance of a man. Therefore it is not possible to abolish the convention of taking suicide to be the ultimate means to restore lost honor without changing the nature of man. That, to be sure, sounds wrong in itself because it sounds as if we would no longer then be dealing with human beings. However, with appropriate qualifications it can be seen to be true; one such qualification is that the nature of human beings is historically determined. We can thus say that it is the *form* of the human that changes, for the form of a thing need not be external to the thing itself.)

Iago, too, knows about this in a rudimentary fashion, or, more accurately, he knows how to talk about it. When he decides to make Othello aware of his feigned suspicion of Cassio and Desdemona, he says,

> Good name in man and woman's dear, my lord;
> Is the immediate jewel of our souls:
> Who steals my purse, steals trash, 'tis something, nothing,
> 'Twas mine, 'tis his, and has been slave to thousands;
> But he that filches from me my good name
> Robs me of that which not enriches him,
> And makes me poor indeed.

(3.3.159–65)

In fact Iago says nothing that Othello himself does not know, insofar as Othello knows anything about such things. Rather, he intimates to Othello that he, Iago, knows about the importance of reputation too. At the same time Iago lets Othello know that he, Iago, is conscious of the responsibility he now bears: if his remarks about Cassio turn out to be untrue, he can be called to account for them.

23. Calling a person a schemer is a serious charge, particularly if it is done within earshot of others. If we have a good reputation, we have it in the eyes of those who make up the "general public." We cannot have a good (or bad) reputation in our own eyes. The charge of being a schemer will destroy our good reputation if that charge is regarded as justified. Conversely, if the person making the charge is not believed, he may easily appear in turn as a schemer. Of course Goethe's dictum that there is no human crime to which we cannot feel a disposition in ourselves does not mean that everybody is guilty of every offense. (Here, by the way, is the germ of my reflections in the next chapter.)

Seen in this light, it is remarkable that we can call someone a disgusting schemer. For, if we take the comment "You are a schemer" as our yardstick, "You are a disgusting schemer" will sound strange, as it invites us to ask whether a schemer can *fail* to be disgusting. Could he even be *pleasant*?

24. An attribute such as "disgusting" does not simply indicate the possibility of a higher degree of scheming, which in turn suggests the possibility of a lower degree, so that gradually one might in the end be led to some

minimal positive moral recognition. But it points toward something similar. Schemes and schemers are subject to evaluation in more than one respect. For instance, we call some people "master" schemers. This contains at least a modicum of admiration. In some cases it is even the point of the statement.

Since such a statement can arise out of admiration, it is also possible to say to somebody's face that he is a master schemer, without wishing to hurt, let alone destroy, him. It is then just an expression of respect and recognition, the kind of praise that will support and build up the admired individual. As far as possible, with the appropriate modifications, this is also valid for actions. An example is provided by Bertolt Brecht in his *Arbeitsjournal* (Work Diary) on 26 January 1941:

> H[ella] W[uolijoki] wanted *Puntila* . . . for the competition of Finnish dramatists; submitted it to the committee but got no prize. Reason seems to me: she did not do any scheming.[14]

Why didn't she? One answer, which interests us here only insofar as it is one possible and relevant response to the question, is this: she did not want to soil her hands; she wanted to preserve her innocence.

Brecht's remark sounds like a sober observation, but it contains a note of regret. This becomes particularly clear when he continues: "as if it were not precisely the good that needs advertising, string pulling, and scheming most." Here something essential is revealed about the schemer: he proceeds in a certain way that is character-

---

[14] B. Brecht, *Arbeitsjournal* 1938–1955, ed. W. Hecht (Berlin: Aufbau, 1977), p. 148 (our translation).

istic of him, but at the same time he also pursues a certain purpose, or motive, that becomes a relevant factor in the moral evaluation of his actions. (Macbeth, for example, clearly has such a purpose in mind; Richard III even more so—and in both cases our judgment of the moral value of their purposes plays a significant part in our attitude to them.) To say that a person is a schemer stresses the procedure, but does not entirely leave the motive and the result out of account. This is reflected in the possible reactions to the accusation of scheming, which include pointing out the purpose and circumstances of the scheme with the intention of at least partially justifying it.

Therefore the possibility of justifiable admiration for the schemer derives from at least two sources:

1. his coolheadedness, his circumspection, his readiness to take risks, his skill in dissimulation, his ability to judge human nature, or a special mixture of all these and whatever else a master schemer needs; and

2. the fact that no particular harm has been done or, if it has, it was too long ago or too far removed from our concerns, or it was offset by a great good, or at least something good came out of it, a greater evil was prevented, or the like.

In the master schemer we admire properties, faculties, and achievements that we also admire in others and in them possibly without reservation. The fact that in the schemer we admire them with reservations does not mean that we do not admire them at all. Rather, we conditionally transfer an attitude to the mastery of a technique that is composed of the above-mentioned properties, faculties, and achievements. The technique itself it is not entirely free of any purpose of any kind, but, since it can be applied to various purposes, it is free of any *specific* one. However, some purposes can at times be achieved only by means of this or that specific technique. Many good things have the property that they can be achieved only if they are brought about by good people.

25. Where something is achieved, there was previously struggle. Where a struggle is taking place, there is often room for craftiness. And the road from craftiness to scheming is only a short one. Given that we can hardly expect the opponents of the good to play fair, are some schemers heroes?

To put this so baldly would amount to an abuse of language. Naturally, there is a difference. It is not the case that our hands remain clean if we scheme in a just cause. In fact, we then will still be sullied among the nations. Nor is this dirt comparable to an honorable scar that we have sustained in an open struggle for a just cause, because the struggle was not conducted openly. Even if the struggle could not be conducted openly, or could certainly not have been won if conducted openly, we cannot simply say that the greater the good and the clearer it is that it could be achieved only by scheming, the more our wound, or the stain on our waistcoat, resembles a well-earned medal. If anything, that stain may be said to reflect badly on a world in which we can help the good to prevail only by such means. But the fact that the world is bad does not make us look good; it only makes us look *relatively* good—or it abolishes the grounds on which such judgments can be made.

Awareness of this state of affairs expresses itself in various ways. One is the schemer's regret for his own deeds. Even if, were the same situation to recur, he would do what he has done again, he would not enjoy it. Or if he enjoys it, he does so with a bitter aftertaste. He may enjoy doing what he does, but only in that way in which we may with reservations admire his skill. The schemer's awareness of this also informs his attitude to those he uses as means to his ends, that is, as mere objects. Once the deed is done and his new scheme is safe, he once again turns back to those "objects" in a way that one can only describe as "human." In so doing he shows that, even from the beginning, those affected by his actions were not mere objects to him. As for the others, one expression of their consciousness of the ambiguity of this moral situation is that they rarely praise the master schemer in public. Thus Brecht, too, voices the above criticism only in his work diary. If it were possible to praise a schemer publicly, "schemer" would not be a term of abuse. But it is one, and as far as public morality is concerned, the schemer enters the stage as a prima facie sinister fellow, albeit one who may hope for soft lighting.

26. One indication of the difference between a wily individual and a schemer is the presence of intermediary links through which we can move in thought from the one to the other. Links connect different kinds of things, not the same kind of things. Such links include the conspirator and the paternalist. Clarifying the differences in this way as differences will also throw light on the peculiarity of Iago's nature.

I said above that Othello is a kind of counterpart of Iago. So is the paternalist, but in a different respect.

If we act in the interests of another person, we must often keep quiet about it, not only to third persons but even to the person directly affected, or else we run the risk of not being able to realize those interests. In many cases that is no problem. For example, not only may small secrecies, such as those that are sometimes needed to prepare a pleasant surprise, be harmless; in some cases it might be reprehensible to betray them. There are, of course, cases where the stakes are high, but we have more or less acceptable reasons to believe that the beneficiary would approve of our actions if only he were not so obstinate, or that he may even be waiting for us to do something that he is unable to do, and that finally he will be glad and thank us for not letting him in on the plan of action. There are all kinds of possible variations, which are difficult to judge and which may therefore give us cause to act on behalf of the person concerned behind his back. In these cases we are forced to give specific reasons for our actions, which are, therefore, not neutral, let alone good in themselves. If we are finally unable to adduce *any* reasons, we expose ourselves to *unconditional* censure.

We need to have special reasons not to inform those affected by our interventions on their behalf. That is just another way of saying that individuals have a right to know about those actions of others that directly affect their lives. How else could it be if there is such a thing as the right of the individual to self-determination?

To the paternalist this is at best of only secondary interest. He is primarily, or exclusively, concerned with what he, often rightly, believes to be in the interests of the other person. That is, self-determination is something the paternalist hardly realizes is essential and close to the heart of the other. There is a certain irony in this, if we consider how easily our attitude to another person can appear as indifference, how narrow the ridge is between the paternalist who is really concerned with the (potentially reduced) welfare of the other, and the paternalist who is primarily concerned with himself and especially gratified by the idea that whatever (halfway) good has been done was done by *him*. It is precisely in this way that he resembles Iago, although he is radically different from him in his attitude toward the welfare of others. Through his actions, the paternalist (potentially) disempowers those to whom he wants to do good. He treats others— hence the term—as certain fathers treat their children, when they are actually no longer children.

In this sense the title "paternalist" appears not to be a morality-laden one, as it is not accompanied by a clear, unequivocal evaluation. To call somebody a paternalist means neither to blame nor to praise him. To say that calling someone a "paternalist" is not to make a moral judgment on him does not mean that moral considerations are irrelevant. It means that two distinct kinds of moral considerations apply, but that they, as it were, neutralize each other. The paternalist, on the one hand, desires the good of the person whom he treats as a child. On the other hand, the paternalist also wishes to be the one who produces the good of the "child," thereby denying the child his autonomy.

If there is such a thing as a right to self-determination, then for *conceptual* reasons the paternalist infringes it. When the paternalist says he wants what is best for, say, John, this may not be false, but "what is best for John" may mean very different things in the mouth of the paternalist and in John's mouth. For the paternalist it means that he knows of some state of affairs that would, in his view, be "objectively" best for John, and he proposes, or even tries, to produce this state. For John, in contrast, "what is best for John" may mean what is "objectively" optimal, but it may also mean what *he*, John, wants, simply because he wants it, whatever that turns out to be. In the second case, if John does get what he wants, but it does him more harm than good, he will be less aggrieved than someone would be who was primarily interested in his own well-being, regardless of how it was brought about. In contrast, the paternalist is unable to attach a great deal of importance to something simply because another, with a will of his own, wants it. That is what he means when he says that he knows what the other *really* wants because he knows what is good for him. To put it positively: he shows signs of a certain concern and thoughtfulness. The two factors, considered in abstract terms, more or less neutralize each other. But that is precisely what one cannot say about Iago, because—to phrase it in a deliberately lopsided way—he lacks anything to put on one side of the balance.

It is obvious that paternalists cannot, without denying themselves, rub shoulders with those for whom self-determination is important and in whose view the good cannot lie beyond what they regard as good. (Thus, in a certain sense, they recognize no difference between something *being* good and something being *regarded* as good; or, if they do recognize a difference, they do not consider it generally valid.) If we recognize the right to self-determination, we must (be able to) efface ourselves. That is precisely what the paternalist, by definition, cannot do. (To him, the difference between what *is* good and what is *regarded* as good goes hand in hand with an exaggerated confidence in his own judgment in contrast to the fallibility of others, when it comes to recognizing what is really good.) The paternalist can't help himself; he must intervene. To the extent that *covert* conflicts, as opposed to overt ones, are less dangerous, he is, however, also less at risk of himself being harmed by his intervention. This may be welcome to the paternalist, but is only a side effect and not an essential feature of his situation. Those who act covertly primarily out of fear are cowards; but a paternalist need not be a coward, although on the other hand a cowardly paternalist is not a contradiction in terms.

What militates in favor of the paternalist, perhaps above all else, is the difficulty that any sympathetic and well-meaning individual will experience if he must watch another rush headlong into disaster. If being master of his own destiny is important for a certain person, this makes it easier for him to cope with suffering, so long as it is only the result of what he wanted to do or did willingly. But he suffers, all the same. The more the right to self-determination is construed to mean not just that I get to decide what happens to me, but also that I bring it about, the less room there is for a paternalist to act in his characteristic way. The paternalist must learn that the failure to achieve what he takes to be the objectively best outcome need not be the worst of all disasters, although it still might be undesirable. In all these respects we may know better than the actor himself—but we must let him go *his* way, in accordance with his need for self-determination, if we do not want to be paternalistic. (As far as our own children are concerned, this is almost unbearable and, if they are not yet adults, unjustifiable—but in relation to our own children we cannot be paternalists in the strict sense in any case, only "mother hens.")

One of the characteristics of the paternalist is his insistence on loyalty from the person whose welfare he promotes. However, the purported "loyalty" to which he appeals is not real loyalty but something else, usually some combination of submissiveness and gratitude. Real loyalty requires independence of decision and action, which is not possible when paternalism is in place. For the same reason friendship is incompatible with paternalism. True, in one sense friendship obviously does not presuppose equality: it is no contradiction to say that the head of government is friendly with his driver. But in another sense, which needs no explanation, it definitely does. This does not make friendship in the former sense an illusion, but neither does it leave it entirely unaffected. What it suggests is that friendship must assume a specific *form* in the face of the given social conditions, as expressed, for example, in Brecht's version of an ancient, anonymous Chinese poem:

> The Friends
>   If you came riding in a carriage
> and I was wearing a peasant's smock
> and we met one day on the road
> you would get out and bow.

>   And if you were selling water
> and I came riding on a horse
> and we met one day on the road
> I would get down to greet you.[15]

As for the other link I mentioned above, the term "conspirator" has primarily negative connotations. Conspiracy is an offense, and in many cases rightly so. However, we also talk about conspirators, for example, in

---

[15] B. Brecht, Chinesische Gedichte, in B. Brecht, *Werke. Große kommentierte Berliner und Frankfurter Ausgabe*, vol. 11: Gedichte 1, ed. W. Hecht, J. Knopf, W. Mittenzwei, and K.-D. Müller (Berlin: Aufbau; Frankfurt a. M.: Suhrkamp, 1988), p. 257 (our translation).

connection with the events in Germany around 20 July 1944. To have been a conspirator of that kind is a good thing. If we were to generalize, we might say that there are circumstances in which *not* to have been a conspirator is a moral blemish.

Those who conspire do so *against* something—and the important thing is *what* they conspire against. Since the mere fact that a conspiracy exists can be evaluated positively or negatively, what matters more than anything else is what the conspirators conspire against. To that extent the concept of the conspirator differs in kind from the concept of the paternalist and that of the schemer. It is not a concept of a type of character.

If we know that a person is a conspirator but not what he is conspiring against and with whom, we know too little to make a well-founded moral judgment about that person. If we nevertheless pass a moral judgment, a negative one implies that we see no special reason to depart from our usual tacit default assumption that the conspiracy is against something that does not deserve to be the target of a conspiracy.

In the case of scheming, the emphasis shifts more toward the principle "That is never really allowed." This is, of course, not a principle that applies without exception. The sentence stands for a conditional prohibition, while the conspirator sees it rather as the sign "Beware—Danger Zone." If the concept of *prima facie duty* has any justifiable application, it is to the avoidance of scheming.[16]

---

[16] See W. D. Ross, *The Right and the Good* (Oxford: Oxford University Press, 1930; reprint, Indianapolis: Hackett, 1988), pp. 18ff. Incidentally, Ross regards this expression, quite rightly, as a terminological stopgap.

27. Instead of saying that scheming is a conditionally forbidden activity, we may say, as I have already done, that *pure* scheming is forbidden. By saying this, we have created a conceptual space for two kinds of schemes: to talk about a pure X is meaningful only where one can also talk about an *impure* X.

This manner of speaking is useful in that it indicates that pure scheming is structurally poorer than impure scheming. However, it is also misleading in that it creates the impression that pure scheming is ontologically primary to impure. The impure, so the image goes, is the pure *plus* something else that contaminates it when added. Without the pure, then, there is no impure. Wherever we have the impure, we also have the pure, albeit not as such. This image, however, does not apply in our case, because pure scheming is either an abstraction or an exception to the rule. The concrete, or the rule, is impure scheming. (Pure scheming is a *privation* of impure scheming.) Just because something contains less than something else, it is not ontologically primary. A common frog is not "really" a three-legged frog plus a fourth leg. Rather, the four-legged frog is the ontologically primary, and the three-legged one is defective, a pathological case, in fact a privation. Among schemers the pure ones are the exception, not the rule.

Pure scheming, then, is scheming liberated from the purpose and the result of the actions to which it lends its form. The pure schemer is one who has the tendency to bring about *every* state of affairs that he tries to bring about . . . by scheming. Provided, of course, that the condition that is to be produced at all lends itself to being produced by scheming. (Is it possible to open a window by scheming, as opposed to opening the window as part of a scheme?) The method of bringing the desired state about, the mode of proceeding, or whatever one may wish to call it, has become independent. It is no longer controlled by the purpose, as it usually is.

It could be objected that if what some say, and many believe, is true, in politics pure scheming is the rule rather than the exception. And once we have taken this route, it is easy to find further areas to which the same would apply. So the thesis that pure scheming is exceptional is either wrong or at any rate not valid for every area of our lives. It is correct that a vice that presents itself in such and such conditions in such and such a way may present itself differently in different conditions, and that the way it presents itself in any particular instance can be decisive for what it is—its nature. This is an important aspect of our idea of a panopticon. In the case of pure scheming, however, things look rather different. Those who believe that politicians are a bunch of pure schemers either do not know what they are saying or are measuring these agents by the wrong yardstick. In comparison with what is common elsewhere, this judgment might seem to have much to recommend it; but only if one considers the action of a politician in isolation and not within the framework in which by its nature it belongs. This framework is characterized by the use of all kinds of tricks in pursuit of certain aims. What would be a scheme within the circle of friends, family, or colleagues, in the political framework is the rule and therefore no scheme. The schemer exploits the trust of his fellow humans. But a politician who trusts another politician blindly is naive and therefore a bad politician, while someone who does not trust a friend is a bad friend or indeed no friend at all. Often those who want so-called honest politics want no politics at all—that is, conditions in which one cannot meaningfully talk about the use of collective human power to pursue important interests. Or they want a kind of politics that is radically different from any politics we know from human history. A "realistic" politics must also provide space for "carefully considered trust." Comparing trust in politics with the form of trust that is customary in friendships, we cannot manage without inverted commas here. But the fact that we cannot manage without them does not mean that we cannot talk about trust in politics at all. We can talk about it, but in a special sense. Admittedly, the sense in which we talk about trust in friendship is also a specific one, not simply trust as such. If things were different, there could hardly be all those innumerable tragic situations in which we encounter a friend in his role as a politician or in which politicians try to be friends.

Incidentally, it is not necessary to express moral doubts about the whole domain of politics in such terms. Nevertheless, some deep moral reservation might be appropriate. Human beings would not normally be able to tolerate a life of nothing but politics as it is currently practiced without being damaged. It is often inappropriate to criticize behavior in one sphere of human life on the grounds that it does not meet the standards that prevail in another. Criticism of this kind need not imply that the first domain ought not to exist at all. Despite all this, there is still a significant difference between saying that a sphere of human life ought not to exist and remonstrating with an individual for doing something that he should not have done.

28. The concept of pure scheming—and accordingly of the pure schemer—brings us close to the concept of Iago.

There are, however, boundaries, even though they are fluid. By characterizing (pure) scheming, we have not yet described Iago's nature. There remains a residue, so to speak, that distinguishes the two. Iago does not merely tend to use schemes in order to achieve his objectives. Rather, whether he achieves one objective rather than another is of only marginal interest to him. Scheming, for him, is a passion, rather than a means to an end, and a passion that constitutes his entire being.

This sounds as if Iago were simply a heightened form of the pure schemer, the resublimated or superpure schemer, as we might say. But that is not the case. (If a substance is chemically sublimated, and the sublimation has been successful, it cannot be further sublimated without being destroyed. Once there is only gold left in the crucible, we can further sublimate the liquid substance only by dissolving it in something that is no longer a chemical element or chemical matter.) With Iago it is not the case that something more has been subtracted from the garden-variety schemer, leaving only one thing behind, but rather that as a result of an omission something that we all know has been shifted from its customary position to a completely different one. The problem is that its customary relative position constitutes what it *is*, just as being the superior of an ensign is part of what it is to be a general. Therefore we cannot simply say that what for others is a means, for Iago becomes the end. Where Iago is concerned, "end" does not have the usual meaning, which contrasts it with "means." If we speak of an end in the normal sense, we can ask by what means it is to be attained. With reference to Iago that question is inappropriate.

To a certain extent, then, Iago is a sublimation, and thus an intensification, of something familiar, which is why Shakespeare was able to write his play and we are able to understand it. But in another respect Iago is something utterly extraordinary, which is why we cannot make any *direct* use of Shakespeare's play in our lives. There is a sense in which the concept of Iago is too smooth to be handled in daily life, and the evil embodied in him is too evil really to fit something natural. As Othello says,[17] Iago is a demi-devil, that is, half fallen angel, but above all else also half superhuman.

29. If Othello recognizes the demi-diabolical element in Iago, he does so by directly encountering it, certainly not because he comprehends it. Othello senses what Iago is about, but he has no concept of him. His picture of Iago, which is based on what he notices about him, is definitely not a manifestation of a particular capability for conceptualizing. Othello has no such capability in relation to Iago. Or, if he has, it is different from, say, Shakespeare's and again different from what we are trying to acquire here. Othello's views about Iago, then, become understandable precisely if they are *not* understood as a manifestation of his powers of ratiocination. Or, if they can be understood as such, reason is a much wider concept than we can picture it if we restrict ourselves to the colors found on the palette of most philosophers. If we restrict ourselves to these colors, we may be able to paint

---

[17] See the line preceding 5.2.302, quoted above. Bloom, *Shakespeare*, p. 643, is not satisfied with "demi-devil": he believes that Iago is "the perfect Devil of the West." Bradley, *Shakespearean Tragedy*, p. 208, writes that only Mephisto bears comparison with Iago. However, while Iago knows no purposes but only methods, Mephisto, so to speak, knows only purposes—evil—and no methods, which results in his wanting evil but always creating good in the process.

a picture only of what is *not* the case. Othello's views about Iago are what they are, not because Iago reveals to Othello something that Othello's reason then makes him believe. On the contrary, Othello finally recognizes Iago without ever acquiring a concept of him. The fact that he enables *us* to acquire such a concept neither suffices to deny him any recognition of Iago nor compels us to credit him merely with a parasitic recognition, nourished by our own. It is true, however, that Othello's real purpose in life is to provide us with a peculiar insight into Iago.

We can understand what drives Iago by sharing Othello's suffering and by reminding ourselves of what I described above (section 12) as something that, from a distance, perhaps looks like a motive for Iago but is not one. Here is once more the crucial passage from Iago's harangue of Roderigo:

> others there are,
> Who, trimm'd in forms, and visages of duty,
> Keep yet their hearts attending on themselves,
> And throwing but shows of service on their lords,
> Do well thrive by 'em, and when they have liv'd in their
>   coats,
> Do themselves homage, those fellows have some soul,
> And such a one do I profess myself, . . . for sir,
> It is as sure as you are Roderigo,
> Were I the Moor, I would not be Iago.

That Iago would not be Iago if he were the Moor is obvious. He would be Othello. We may assume that Othello does not want to be Iago. Does that mean that Iago would not want to be Iago if he were the Moor? Perhaps because Othello, if he were Iago, would have to perform Iago's "shows of service" in order to achieve what he would

want to achieve if he were Iago? Does Iago therefore
simply suffer from an inner conflict as a result of having
to be different from what he would like to be, in order
to obtain what, being what he is, he wants to obtain? It
seems to me that this would underrate Iago's intellect and
make his character appear too close to an ordinary one.
What Iago means in this passage is something different.
He suggests a difference between himself and Othello
that, in his eyes, is greater than the difference between
Othello and Cassio or between Othello and Desdemona,
indeed greater than the difference between *any* two people, as that difference is usually understood.

According to the usual understanding of that difference, it makes sense to say that Iago *could* be in Othello's
place. Had things taken a different course, Iago could be
the general and Othello his ensign. Had things developed
differently, Desdemona would be Iago's wife and Emilia
Othello's. Indeed we can imagine all kinds of scenarios
in which Iago would be in Othello's place. The more
such scenarios we imagine, the more we find ourselves in
a position in which it sounds almost natural to say that
Iago is not Iago but Othello. And if that can sound natural, so can a sentence like "If Iago were Othello, he
would want to be Iago." Othello could wish to be Iago,
even if he has not yet reached that point. That, I think, is
the sense in which Iago would *not* want to be Iago if he
were Othello.

30. The difference Iago has in mind is a fundamental one
in that it precludes the possibility of meaningfully saying
that one person could be in the position of another. And
where that is pointless, it is also pointless for one person
to want to be another.

This difference is so great that it relegates the boundary between Iago and all other people—that is, the essential boundary that also exists between each of us and all others—to the background. To the extent that this boundary is a universal one, separating me in each case from *all* others, it puts all those others together into a single category. Thus Iago does not violate a boundary that he recognizes as such. If that were the case, he would need to be prepared to defend his actions before himself and selected others. In fact, he gives no indication that he thinks he has any need to defend himself in any way. It seems he simply does not recognize that boundary at all. That is what distinguishes him from the schemer, who is essentially linked to other people whom he recognizes as other people through his motives, which make sense only if other people are separate agents, who can sometimes be influenced and manipulated.

The difference between Iago and the others is, for Iago, the quintessential boundary. There is a sense in which everything outside himself is, in comparison with himself, all of a piece. For Iago, the difference between himself and Othello is of the same kind as that between himself and Cassio, while the difference between Cassio and Othello is of a quite distinct, almost trivial kind. (See the reference to 3.4.101–3 above.) That is what makes the former the quintessential boundary. Most people make a distinction between themselves and others, but they also distinguish between humans and nonhumans, and this second distinction is of some importance to them. For Iago, on the other hand, these two distinctions rather merge into one, so that for him there is no essential difference between the different kinds of things, human and nonhuman, that are not himself.

For Iago, the only difference is that between himself
and everything else, whatever that may be. (In this sense
Bloom's remark about war as Iago's true element acquires
a new, as it were metaphysical, meaning.) By standing out
against all other things in this way, Iago sets them an
absolute boundary and in so doing defines them. For
himself, Iago is the measure of all things. While for all of
us ordinary people the human—in which we participate,
but which does not coincide with any of us—provides
the standard by which we regard good as good and evil as
evil, for Iago the only standard is himself. Consequently,
where he is concerned, we cannot talk about a standard
in the common sense of the word. For a standard is not
located in the individual. If it were, the individual would
have the discretion to choose whether or not to meet it,
and this would mean it was not really a standard. Whatever Iago believes to be the standard, however, is supposed to be the standard because he believes it to be. But
such a thing is no human standard.

This is directly conveyed by the fact that the concept of
a good name means nothing to Iago, even though he
"knows" (see section 22) what it means to *us*. He counters
Cassio's lament over the loss of his good reputation as
follows:

> As I am an honest man, I thought you had receiv'd some
> bodily wound, there is more offence in that than in rep-
> utation: reputation is an idle and most false imposition,
> oft got without merit, and lost without deserving. You
> have lost no reputation at all, unless you repute yourself
> such a loser. (2.3.257–63)

Whether or not I have lost my good reputation is inherently not the kind of thing I can decide by myself. If a

good reputation can be "oft got without merit, and lost without deserving," it must also be possible to get it with merit and to lose it with deserving. But what it *is* in any one case, whether obtained with or without merit, cannot be decided by every individual at will.

Cassio's view that a person's moral standing is deeply connected with his reputation contains an important grain of truth. Morality itself would be abolished if we could all decide for ourselves whether we have this or that reputation. When it comes to Iago, we either cannot talk about morality at all, or as far as we can—since a phrase such as "Iago's morality" does not seem to be meaningless—it is a morality that is different from the usual kinds.

31. Here the dual nature of our approach is once more revealed. On the one hand, think of Iago's actions as displayed in full array. Then it is clear that a person who behaves in such a way that his actions could be integrated more or less seamlessly into that display behaves villainously, just as, for example, something is a fungus if in terms of appearance, structure, and the like it can be seamlessly integrated into the array of fungi. This constitutes the unequivocally moral element. On the other hand, we have already seen that Iago embodies an open behavioral pattern that is pathological in nature. This constitutes the extramoral.

Where the immediate effect of the play is concerned, there can be no question as to Iago's morality or, rather, immorality. However, if the interpretation presented here is plausible, this immediate reaction should remain problematic as a *fully* adequate response to the play so long as it does not bring with itself a further reaction.

This further reaction should consist, in part at least, in recognizing that Iago, among other things, draws attention to some significant issues that arise from the very concept of moral evaluation.

That the members of the audience at a particular performance have no more than the simple immediate reaction to the play is not in itself problematic, since a play is not an ethical tract, and being part of the audience at the performance of the play is not an exercise in moral philosophizing either. This also corresponds to what was said earlier (section 29) about the way Othello finally recognizes Iago for what he is without forming a particular concept of Iago. As far as this kind of recognition, or not explicitly conceptualized knowledge, has an independent value, it is not in any way deficient. But the fact that knowledge, if it is to be knowledge, need not have the form it takes in these tracts, if it is to be counted as an expression of knowledge, is also no argument against the tracts.

If the results of this interpretation seem to run counter to the effect I called "immediate," this raises problems of its own. I will begin with those, before returning to our central theme. In the process we shall see that the immediate reaction to Iago should not be replaced with another, but that, as a further reaction joins the first, something new comes into being in which the old still retains a rightful place.

CHAPTER TWO

Apologia for Iago

2.1. DEFENSE, JUSTIFICATION, AND UNDERSTANDING

32. "Apologia" means, roughly, defense or justification. Generally, we defend people, institutions, and various other things, while we justify patterns of behavior, reflections, intentions, feelings, and the like. However, people or institutions, on the one hand, and actions, thoughts, or intentions, on the other, are not completely separate spheres. There is no action, no thought, no intention, no feeling without a person acting, thinking, intending, or feeling. Conversely, if we want to know the person we are dealing with, we must look at what he does, thinks, intends, and feels. The connections between people and their behavior, people and their thoughts, and so forth, are ontologically on a par with the connections between the defense of people and the justification of their actions, and the like.

There is a second sense in which defense and justification are different but connected. They are different insofar as we can defend a person without justifying his actions. To put it another way, there is no contradiction in saying, "His behavior cannot be justified, but let me defend him all the same." But even though that statement does not contain a contradiction, it calls for an explanation. What, then, might a defense that is no justification look like? We could, for example, tell a story that made it difficult not to accept that there were mitigating circumstances, not to temper justice with mercy, or even not to remove the whole event from the perspective of right or wrong.

The connection between defense and justification is shown by the form of words I have just used. We do not say, for example, "Joe Bloggs's daughter is good at maths, but Joe Bloggs's car is red." If we did, we would naturally ask ourselves what the color of Joe Bloggs's car had to do with his daughter's intelligence. By asking that question, we would have tacitly acknowledged a connection between the two, and the analogous structure of the statement quoted in the previous paragraph reveals a similar connection between defense and justification.

What follows is meant to be a defense but *not* a justification. Therefore, if it is successful as a defense, it will be a justification only as far as the two cannot be separated.

33. Wanting to defend something usually presupposes the belief that it is in need of defense. For this to happen, it must be the subject of an accusation.

In Iago's case the existence of an accusation cannot be denied. To call someone "an Iago" is more than just a stronger form of calling him a schemer. And that, as I have suggested, is one of the worst things that can be said about a person.

APOLOGIA FOR IAGO 79

A defense is not the same as a justification, although a defense can of course *consist* of a justification, as the following exchange may indicate: "How do you intend to defend him?" "By showing that he did the right thing." The reason why I intend to defend Iago but not to justify him is that he cannot be justified. For him there is no defense that consists of a justification. There *cannot* be.

We see why there cannot be such a defense if we recall what a justification is. The proof that there cannot be is the strongest confirmation of the feeling that it would be absurd to assume that all those could be wrong who, as Johnson puts it (see quotation above), hate and despise Iago from the first scene. It is absurd because they all do. If it is indeed right that my reputation is something that exists in the eyes of others, then the consensus opinion on Iago could not be wrong. (Of course, it could be wrong if the *times* to which that consensus belongs are special— which simply is a different case.) The immediate reaction is a reaction, then, that *determines* what is worthy of hatred or contempt.

To justify something, to put it crudely and a little imprecisely, is to trace it back to something right, in such a way that the rightness is inherited by the object of the justification. This can easily be misunderstood because it sounds very much like reductionism. But that is not the fault of the formulation. Formulations in themselves are never at fault. The important thing is the way we use them, how we intend them, what we immediately think of when we hear them, and so forth. Here the formulation is expressly not meant to be reductionist.

Why cannot Iago be justified? Because he appears as the ultimate, absolute schemer. As such, he is a particularly transcendent figure. In this case all possible extenuating motives have already dropped away. It is not the case that once in a while he weakens and does something evil that does not reflect his nature in a pure form. Rather, he expresses himself fully in every image of the panopticon that the play presents to us. Thus he is not simply a wicked individual who could just as easily be good. He is a *paradigm* of evil, the villain *as such*—as far as there are paradigms of evil and villainy. To put it differently, Iago embodies the concept of evil, or, more precisely, he belongs in the ranks of those who embody that concept.

However, in the precise degree in which Iago is regarded as the embodiment of evil, he is removed from the perspective of moral evaluation. A model of evil itself cannot be evaluated and therefore cannot be justified or, for that matter, fail to be justified. So long as we cling to the method of measuring by the standard meter, we cannot measure the length of the standard meter. How could we? If we nevertheless call Iago a villain—that is, if we call evil itself "evil"—we are stressing that something that cannot strictly be called evil does not have to be morally neutral, let alone good. Here, too, the following model is used: those who behave in the opposite way to Iago are good; those who behave neither like Iago nor like his opposite are neutral. (Similarly, we might say that a color card we use, for example, to define "green" is . . . green. It seems that as it is not colorless, it must have a color; and what color could that be if not green? Or are we to believe that it is possible to use a blue color card to define "green"? It is not clear at first sight what is going wrong here.) If it has to be one or the other of two, good is good and not evil, justice is just and by no means unjust, virtue is virtuous and never vicious, and so on.

But, strictly, we cannot call even good itself "good." We can judge something as good and thereby justify it. We can judge something as evil and thereby condemn it, but good and evil themselves elude evaluation and therefore also justification. We can only try to *understand* them.

At this point it should be clear that we are dealing with the *concept* of Iago and not with Iago as an individual. Earlier I briefly considered Bloom's idea of seeking Iago's motivation in the prehistory of the play as far as it can be reconstructed from hints in the text. That approach may be ethically relevant, where the evaluation of a person, in contrast to the evaluation of an action, is at issue. The reason for this is that we sometimes distinguish between people in terms of behavior patterns that are either typical or untypical of them, and to know what kind of behavior is typical of them means to know something about their history. This distinction preserves the essential continuity of action and person, by binding a person's character essentially to what he habitually does. However, the distinction should not be indiscriminate but should differentially reflect the particular circumstances in which different actions were performed. In other words, the behavior of a person can be classified according to the matrix "rule—exception." To establish what is the rule and what the exception, one must know a sufficiently large variety of different actions he performed in identical circumstances, or of identical actions in different circumstances. The difficulty is to avoid running ahead of the evidence and precipitously construing a certain sort of actions as exhibiting some preconceived pattern when the existence of any such pattern is precisely as yet unclear. But this does not mean that it is never possible to recognize any patterns.

Another method of distinguishing between action and person comes into play if we decide that the *actions* of a person are not reprehensible because he was unable to act in any other way. Here many different cases are imaginable. One of them allows us to evaluate the *person* concerned according to whether or not he was responsible for the condition in which he could no longer act in any other way than he did. We are responsible for our actions if we are able to act differently. (If we are not able to act differently, this does not free us of all responsibility for our unscrupulous actions. In some cases we may not think it is exactly right that the agent is responsible for acting unscrupulously—he may have no choice, given who he is. Rather, the proper charge is that the agent is an unscrupulous person. At this point, there is a transition from unscrupulousness as a property of actions to unscrupulousness as a property of a person.) Nevertheless, if we persist in acting unscrupulously, we may become incapable of doing anything else, and we may be left with no conscience. Once we have seen that such a transformation is possible, there is nothing to prevent us from realizing that one person can always have been what another has only become through change. This again could give us the idea that it is always possible to ignore the *genesis* of a person and concentrate instead on his *being*. If we consider this in isolation, it seems that we could never be responsible for our actions. Since a person's actions spring from his being, he can be responsible for his actions only as far as he is responsible for his being, that is, for being the person he is. But that is something for which we cannot in general be responsible, because in order to be responsible we would have had to *choose* to be the persons we are.

However, just as our actions spring from our being, our choice also springs from what we are. To be able to act at all, we must be persons; as soon as we are particular, individuated persons at all, our actions are determined; even if we can choose what persons to be, this choice is again only an expression of who we are; therefore we cannot be responsible for being the persons we are; and therefore we can never be responsible for our actions. If this argument is correct, the advice that is sometimes given—"If you want to know who a person is, study what he *does*, not what he *says* about himself"—is pointless. This suggests that the former tells one more about who a person is than the latter. But if our actions spring from our being, what we say about ourselves tells just as much about us as what we do, because talking about ourselves is also an action. That advice reminds us, not that when we talk about ourselves we are not acting, but that we do not always live up to the image we draw of ourselves. This image varies. Sometimes it reveals how we really see ourselves, at other times how we would like to be, at yet other times how we think it would be advantageous to us to appear to others at any given moment, and so forth. Since drawing such images is itself an activity, it springs from our being exactly as does every other action. Assuming that the advice in question is good advice—which it doubtless is—there must be a difference between talking about ourselves and our other actions, regardless of whether or not all our actions spring from our being. Such a difference, of course, exists: it is the difference between what we want to be and what our strength or circumstances allow us really to be. As we have already seen in our consideration of the schemer, in evaluating him it is important to note whether his actions correspond to how he wants to act or how he feels he has to act in order to get what he wants. In other words, it makes a difference whether we are faced with a pure or an "impure" schemer. It is an empirical fact that a person who is constantly induced to scheme, and who gives in to this inducement, can easily become a pure schemer, so that scheming becomes second nature to him. If this development occurs gradually, he does not choose his later state of being at any one particular previous point. Therefore, on the above argument, he is not responsible for it. But insofar as he was able to know that permanent scheming could change his being, just as constant exercise will enlarge a muscle, he has behaved in a way he should not have done. With regard to his earlier state of being, both alternatives were within his power, and, to that extent, we can say that he did choose. If finally he cannot help doing what he does, he cannot be regarded as guilty, since one condition of guilt is the ability to have acted differently. Similarly, if he has no conscience left, he cannot be judged as guilty by the standards usually applied to unprincipled actions. Nevertheless, he will not escape unscathed and will still have reason—albeit perhaps no longer the ability—to be ashamed, because to some extent it was in his power not to become what he now is. (This is another of those cases in which it is not true that Ought implies Can.) We are not always innocent of being what, or who, we are. Perhaps not even in the majority of cases, and at any rate most of the time not completely.

Naturally, there are also differences in the degree of possible guilt. In those respects in which we can condemn Iago as a person, even if we also admit that his behavior constitutes his nature, we can of course also defend him. It could be that during the formative phase, in which he developed his character into a more or less stable whole, the conditions in which he lived were such that he was able to survive only by behaving as he later does for no external reason. Who would blame him for becoming what he is under such conditions? Can a person who, as a child, was constantly forced to act directly against the palpable interests of others really be blamed for eventually becoming hard-hearted? What more can be meant by "blame" here other than that hard-heartedness is not right, and that it would have been better if the person in question had had a different childhood?

But that is precisely *not* the grounds on which I intend to defend Iago. Nor is it therefore the grounds on which he could be condemned. That is why it is important not to lose sight of the difference between the concept of Iago and Iago himself. In the consideration of that difference, the question how Iago became what he is has no relevance and I will ignore it. We understand Iago as we get to know him in the play, as a person who could in principle have come into being, exactly as he is now, out of nothing. The only thing that concerns us is the *doctrine* he embodies, the *principle* he stands for, the *idea* his actions illustrate.

Therefore the only remaining defense of Iago, as I have said, is to *understand* him. This defense is possible exactly to the same extent as the adage "to understand all is to forgive all" is right. To what extent this is true is determined by how strictly the concept of justification can be separated from that of defense. If they could *not* be separated *at all*, if to understand all just *meant* to forgive and thus to justify all, Austin's objection would be valid: "That can hardly be true; understanding might just add contempt to hatred."[1] The question is what "add" means here. Does understanding a thing we hate *consist* in adding contempt to hatred, or is that addition a *consequence* of the understanding? To the extent that this question makes any sense, it is also possible to separate justification and defense. Furthermore, the stricter such a separation may prove to be, the more the adage about forgiving through understanding can lead to a position in which, by trying to understand something, we leave no room for condemnation or, consequently, for justification either. This position is not simply one further position on the same level as condemnation and justification. Rather, it precedes them in that in order to condemn something, we must have minimally understood it.

On the other hand, the impossibility of a *complete* separation between defense and justification is shown by the fact that our understanding of a thing is also expressed in our evaluative attitude to it. As Elizabeth Anscombe says, "But if someone really thinks, *in advance*, that it is open to question whether such an action as procuring the judicial execution of the innocent should be quite excluded from consideration—I do not want to argue with him; he shows a corrupt mind."[2] Those who understand the court system at all cannot simply keep a low profile when it comes to evaluating a punitive sentence handed down on a person whom the court itself considers to be innocent.

---

[1] Reported by Peter F. Strawson, *Scepticism and Naturalism: Some Varieties* (London: Routledge, 2004), p. 37 n. 5.

[2] "Modern Moral Philosophy," *Philosophy* 32 (1958): 1–19, quotation from p. 17. Incidentally, Anscombe attaches to the phrase "in advance" a footnote discussing whether it is possible to consider such an action. We shall soon see that this thinly veiled inconsistency is not altogether a weakness.

In cases like this, understanding what is happening and evaluating it belong together. Nevertheless, is it really enough to say that those who report the execution of a visibly innocent person without any indignation simply do not know what they are talking about?

Insofar as understanding and judgment, insight and attitude cannot be separated but nevertheless remain distinct, one particular respect in which understanding and forgiving belong together becomes uncommonly interesting. Let us approach this step-by-step.

St. Augustine teaches that "nullumque bonum perfecte noscitur, quod non perfecte amatur."[3] This is by no means a remark about the emotional prerequisites of knowledge. Rather, it is an indication of a special form of knowledge, that is, complete knowledge of the essence of something or, as we may call it, conceptual knowledge. For the concept of a thing is its goodness, in that anything subsumed under a concept becomes the more perfect—in other words, the better—the more it corresponds to the concept. In the ideal case it is as good as it can be—in other words, absolutely good. But how could we not love the good? And how could we recognize something as bad completely without hating it? As Montaigne teaches:

> There is no vice truly a vice which is not offensive, and which a sound judgment (*jugement entier*, R. R.) does not condemn; for its ugliness and painfulness is so apparent that perhaps the people are right who say it is chiefly

---

[3] *De diversis quaestionibus* LXXXII, 35, in *Patrologiae Cursus Completus*, Series Latina (Paris, 1861–1862), 40:24. "No good is completely known which is not completely loved": *Eighty-Three Different Questions*, trans. David L. Mosher (Washington, DC: Catholic University of America Press, 1977), p. 66.

produced by stupidity and ignorance. So hard it is to imagine anyone knowing it without hating it.[4]

The soundness of judgment—what is it if not the attitude we take to what is being judged when we philosophize about it? If we remember that vices are nothing but privations of virtues, that evil is only a perversion of good, and that vices, just like virtues, are the work of man, we are brought directly to the question of the appropriate attitude to man himself and the totality of his actions. In other words, what is that being which is the source of both virtue and vice?

It seems to me that Shakespeare provides an answer to this question, with which St. Augustine and Montaigne would be inclined to agree, the correctness of their remarks about virtue and vice notwithstanding:

> Never durst poet touch a pen to write
> Until his ink were temper'd with Love's sighs;
> O, then his lines would ravish savage ears
> And plant in tyrants mild humility.[5]

We fail to understand not only the bearers of light but also those of darkness unless we love the humanity they share, even if this love is not the same as our love of the good. For if evil is a privation of good, the dark exists only because, and insofar as, there is also the light.

But if we love humanity and are able to know it fully only *in*—not as a *consequence of*—this love, have we not already forgiven those who share it, whatever they may do, simply because they have such a share? Even if they

---

[4] "On Repentance," in *Essais*, p. 612 (note also the speech about the *ugliness* of vice).
[5] W. Shakespeare, *Love's Labour's Lost*, 4.3.322–25.

turn away from it, trying to be like Iago? In fact they cannot do even that without starting from a position of common humanity. Since this must be recognized (in some way or other) if they are to be judged, and it cannot properly be recognized without love, have we therefore not forgiven them exactly in the degree demanded by the love of humanity?

In section 15 I described Iago as an impossibility. What I meant was that he exists beyond the boundary of the human. But he does not exist there in the same way in which this could be said of a stove. A stove is not a pathological case of the human. Iago is precisely that. (The pathological is a form of privation.) To that extent Iago, too, has a share in the human. He falls under this concept and at the same time he does not. This again is compatible with the fact that to some the pathological as represented by Iago appears as nothing but evil and therefore stands outside the realm of humanity. But the concept of evil makes sense only as the opposite of the human good.

34. Let us move on to the details of our case. The defense of Iago that is not his justification places him in a position that is halfway outside morality.

If we say that something is extramoral, we mean, among other things, that it is not an object of moral evaluation, either because it was not so right from the beginning—perhaps the more fundamental form of the extramoral—or because it shows itself eventually to be the kind of thing that eludes the attempt at moral evaluation.

Take the phenomenon of self-defense. I have the right to kill a person if I reasonably believe that he represents an acute and serious threat to my life. Self-defense, of course, is subject to evaluation. I will be asked why I did it. If the reason was the danger to my own life, the action will not be morally condemned outright. Killing a person in self-defense is by no means a good deed, but neither is it an evil one, provided that we presuppose common morality, ignoring those moral systems in which the sanctity of another person's life is paramount. In this case an act of self-defense is extramoral and therefore neither (morally) justified nor (morally) unjustified. It is justified only in the sense that, being made as we are, if our life is threatened we usually do all we can to save ourselves, just as we automatically pull our hand back if it touches a hotplate. Pulling our hand back is not an action, unless we interpret a mere reflexive movement as such. But that does not mean that there is never any continuity between a reflexive movement and an action.

Pulling our hand back from the hotplate is a natural necessity, which stands side by side with our moral impulses, insofar as those, too, are natural, and which sometimes deactivates those impulses. Killing another person in self-defense is generally not a pure reflex but a human act. There are of course some people who would not kill another person even in self-defense. But they are the exceptions. They are superhuman, as it were, in a scientific sense. Those who are not superhuman have reason to regret their fate and perhaps also the fate of the person they had to kill. This regret, however, only *resembles* but is not really a form of moral self-accusation.

Killing in self-defense is an instance of what one might call "human" natural necessity in contrast to the more strict natural necessity of reflex movements. We may say, as I have just done, that an act of self-defense is justified by necessity, but this does not mean that the justification is the same kind of thing as the justification of a good deed in the ordinary sense. To avoid conceptual confusion, I will distinguish between the two types of justification by referring to defense *without* justification in cases of necessity, and to defense *by means of* justification in other cases.

Iago cannot be defended by means of justification. As far as he can be defended, one can do so only by placing his actions in a perspective in which they assume, to some extent, the character of a natural law (albeit one that operates in the realm of real human action).

2.2. DEFENDING IAGO

35. We take the first step in this direction by considering the nature of the human capacity for insight. Although we shall never discover just how we acquired all that we know or believe, it is clear that we acquired a great deal of it merely by being in the right place at the right time. A large proportion of what we know or believe, then, is made up of things that have *befallen* us.

This includes the recognition of opportunities to ensure that this or that comes about, not least those opportunities we are offered by the behavior of others. Thus, for example, an insight into someone else's character goes hand in hand with the realization of how we might induce him to behave in a particular way. Knowing that a person is choleric means knowing that in this or that situation he is likely to react in one way—angrily—rather than in another. We can sometimes bring about such situations either directly by ourselves or indirectly through others, while at other times we need only to wait until they arise of themselves. The same applies to knowing about the situation in which a person finds himself, or about his inclinations, convictions, and values. In short, our entire psychic microcosm consists of opportunities for others. And the insight into this microcosm, with the opportunities it offers, is something that can befall any of us. It simply happens that some people find themselves in a situation in which they know how other people will act.

It could be objected that if perceptions were things that merely befall us, it would be a mystery why some people have a greater gift for observation than others. This Iago is an excellent observer. He is almost as good as de la Rochefoucault, for example, and the reactions to the two of them are similar, although no more than that. De la Rochefoucault is a realist, and what arouses our resistance to him is the firmness with which we cling to illusions, not only about others but also about ourselves, that he relentlessly punctures. But we would not refer to a "gift" for observation if we were dealing only with a chance accumulation of individual perceptions. Being repeatedly hit by the ball and accidentally deflecting it into the goal of the opposition does not make a football player a good scorer. He is simply incredibly lucky. Even if it is true that being a better observer is simply a matter of being more often in the right place at the right time, or even of "producing" the right place and the right time, some further explanation is necessary.

The first point of this objection says only that, for the better observers, more times and more places are the right ones than for less good observers. In the "same" situation good observers see things that others do not see. In that sense, "being in the right place at the right time" is a relational expression. None of that, to be sure,

changes the character of the events that befall us. To say
that something befalls me means that I do not contribute
to it, apart from being there. But it is not quite irrelevant
who or what is there. The fact that Iago is a master observer can only to a very limited extent be considered to
be something meritorious. And if we understand the concept of guilt as the opposite of the concept of merit or
desert, Iago's *guilt*, to the extent to which it is related
to his observational capacities, is similarly limited. However, if Iago is guilty of deceiving him, Othello is corre-
spondingly guilty of being taken in by Iago, and perhaps
of publicly offering something that invites and almost
conjures up the existence of an Iago. The two characters
complement each other even as far as guilt is concerned.

This brings us to the second point. It might be said that
being a better observer can consist in, or at least be as-
sociated with, the ability to create the right time and the
right place, and that this is what should be condemned.
Yes and no. It is true that Iago does all he can to find out
what makes others tick. With regard to the evaluation
of this fact, and this part of the objection, however, we
must take the second step in defense of Iago.

36. I have already hinted at this step in connection with
the problem of the masterly schemer. As far as Iago is
concerned, we need merely to note that it is not the realization of our aims *alone* that can satisfy us. In sports, for
example, as a rule, it is gratifying not only to overcome
our opponent, but also to overcome him *in a specific way*.
Winning does not necessarily mean that we have played
beautifully, just as playing beautifully does not mean that
we have not been defeated. But having played beautifully

can console us in defeat. It is certainly unusual to be more pleased by a beautiful defeat than by an ugly victory, but it is comprehensible, because gratification is not always exclusively due to having completed a job we have begun, but is sometimes due to the process of creation itself. Those who, like the builders of medieval cathedrals, are not granted the pleasure of both beginning a job and seeing it completed have little more than this satisfaction. To say that the work is going well does not mean (only) that it is sure to reach its aim, but can (also) be a judgment about the way it is progressing. ("It's coming along" is an expression of satisfaction, pleasure, enjoyment.) As a rule of thumb, the harder the task, the greater the joy. It is this joy of doing, producing, shaping, inventing—and since living is doing, the joy of life itself—that Iago represents in the pure form: that is, as joy, regardless of what he does, produces, shapes, invents. In this way he lives on in our memory precisely because of his actions.

For Bradley, "Iago's longing to satisfy the sense of power" is "the strongest of the forces that drive him on."[6] The satisfaction is greatest, says Bradley, if we can make others suffer. Why should we not, however, derive just as great a satisfaction from bringing about the happiness of others, as the paternalist does, without involving them as equal or even privileged partners in this process? The satisfaction derived from making others happy seems smaller only because it is not so acute, that is, because it

---

[6] *Shakespearean Tragedy*, p. 230. Bradley contrasts this "longing to satisfy the sense of power," among other things, with "the pleasure in an action very difficult and perilous and, therefore, intensely exciting. This action sets all his powers on the strain" (ibid.). But is it not much more plausible to regard this pleasure as one form of that longing?

does not become immediately conscious, does not hit us in the eye, and does not stimulate our feelings so fast and so abruptly, but rather steadily. If Bradley is right about the force of the attraction issuing from the suffering of others, Iago's behavior appears all the more forgivable, because the temptation issuing from that attraction is also stronger. If, however, we say that the attraction is more acute and not simply stronger, things become more complex and the temptation more than just greater.

Here is the logical place for the attraction of Iago, which we might almost call the beauty of the determined fighter relying only on his own resources. Iago's attraction for us is the same as the attraction to which Iago abandons himself fully, with the difference that we are observers while Iago is an actor. There is a sense in which Iago is the scriptwriter, the director, and the producer of his world. Whatever happens is *his* work—insofar as one can talk about "work" in this context. But Iago is not really an artist, who turns everything around him into his raw material. The artist seeks a goal that essentially connects him with others: dissatisfied with what is recognized as art, he seeks a new form of expression, which he wants to be recognized and accepted into the canon. Iago resembles an artist but is no artist; he denies what could be called, paradoxically, with Hegel, "the root of humanity": "For the nature of humanity is to impel men to agree with one another and its very existence lies simply in the explicit realisation of a community of conscious life."[7] In other words, it is no coincidence that we do

---

[7] G.W.F. Hegel, *Phenomenology of Spirit*, trans. A. V. Miller, with analysis of text and foreword by J. N. Findlay (Oxford: Oxford University Press, 1977), p. 64.

not remember Iago only, or perhaps even primarily, as a
character who pursues wicked intentions and causes in-
credible suffering. With his absolute opposition to everything apart from himself, he can neither find support
nor participate in any commandment or normative order
outside himself. This excessiveness makes him almost in-
human. Our attraction to him is accompanied by a deep
shudder. It is the attraction of the monstrous.

Iago's "individualism" is a case in point. In Heidegger's language, we might say that Iago's "I against the
world" stance is an expression of the fact that he has been
struck by the contingency of everyday existence on realizing that his conventional existence in an essential sense
is not *his* work and to that extent has nothing to do with
him, or that he himself is a nothing. Such an experience is
"able to place Dasein, amid the glory of its everydayness,
into uncanniness"[8]—and that is precisely what surrounds
Iago (for us): the aura of something uncanny. Our reaction to Iago is not only, or not primarily, outrage—the
expression of moral condemnation or at least an element
attendant on it—but, above all else, alarm, that is, the condition that often arises when we become conscious of
the true nature of something very different from anything familiar and very dangerous. If human beings can
do to other human beings what Iago can do to those
around him, what can human beings *not* do to others? And
if human beings allow others to do to them what Othello

---

[8] M. Heidegger, "Der Begriff der Zeit" (lecture, 1924), in *Der
Begriff der Zeit*, Gesamtausgabe, III. Abteilung: Unveröffentlichte
Abhandlungen, Vorträge, Gedachtes, vol. 64, ed. F. W. v. Herrmann
(Frankfurt a. M.: Klostermann, 2004), p. 117. (*The Concept of Time*,
trans. William McNeill [Oxford: Blackwell, 1992], p. 13E.)

allows Iago to do to him, what will human beings *not* allow to be done to them? This alarm resembles the alarm we feel in the face of a force of nature or of fate. But do we ever say that these things "outrage" us except in highly unusual circumstances such as the famous earthquake in Lisbon?

Nevertheless, the fact that in the first place Iago alarms us also means that in the second place we are outraged by him. To put it another way, the difference between those who are primarily outraged and those who are, rather, alarmed by him is not the same as the difference between a person giving information and a person asking for information. The alarm goes hand in hand with the possibility of outrage, whereas we cannot honestly ask for information if we already have it. Our alarm over Iago is related, but not identical, to our alarm over a natural force or fate, in that it does not entirely escape the realm of ethical relevancy. What, however, is this elementary ethical relevance?

Prior to our discussion of Iago's individualism as his main characteristic, we saw him as the scriptwriter, director, and producer of his world, in absolute opposition to whatever comes his way and therefore unable to recognize, and to submit himself and his actions to, any restraint or standard according to the common understanding of the word. In this light, there is no room for Iago *within* the world. He does not belong. His morality therefore accompanies, or indeed consists in, an attitude to the world as a whole. He wants it to be *his* work, if it is to be anything at all. "Demand me nothing, what you know, you know, / From this time forth I never will speak word" are Iago's last words, and Othello, his counterpart, commits suicide. Iago neither justifies his actions, as we

might expect if he were simply wicked, nor does he try
to apologize or to show any traces of repentance, which
would be plausible if he accepted, at least to some extent, the morality by which he is branded as wicked. Instead, he simply shirks all the demands of others. He
does not recognize any demand of the kind, even though,
as was explained above, he knows how to talk about a
good reputation. He uses morality for the purposes of
manipulation—and by so doing, he actually discards it.[9]

Therefore, as has also already been mentioned (see
section 1), Iago is not simply an extreme egoist or, to the
extent that he is one, he changes the concept of egoism. If
egoism is defined as the attitude of a person who is primarily concerned with himself, the only person who can
be an egoist is one who regards others as being situated at
his own level, at least to the extent of considering them to
be possible candidates for pride of place in the hierarchy
of his concerns. The egoist, in everyday language, says, "I
come first, not them." Thus, within his horizon, the
others appear, at least in one respect, as his equals. If we
say that the table is longer than the tablecloth, we have
brought both under the same concept—the concept of
length—without saying that they are of equal length.
Nothing of the kind is true of Iago, or, if it is true, it is
true only with reservations and therefore not true, at least,
with regard to its *tendency*. For those who believe that
morality is always related to the weal and woe of others,
Iago represents a problem, since his way of not caring

[9] See also C. Diamond, "Ethics, Imagination and the Method of
Wittgenstein's *Tractatus*," in *The New Wittgenstein*, ed. A. Crary and
R. Read (London: Routledge, 2000), pp. 149–73, particularly pp.
152ff.

about others is more fundamental than that of the ordinary egoist: while the ordinary egoist at least has some room for others in his head, albeit not in his heart, Iago has no such room anywhere. If, then, he is an amoralist, he is the *absolute* amoralist.

37. If one absolutely insists on trying to stretch our normal forms of moral discourse so that they apply to Iago, for fear that it would otherwise be difficult to condemn him, one might be tempted to try to develop and extend our usual notions of "self-control" so that they give us some moral purchase on Iago. "Self-control" is an important virtue in a number of different contexts, but given the person Iago is, it seems much too weak a demand to impose on him. Iago, after all, is fundamentally constituted by two traits—his preternatural ability to observe and the great pleasure he takes in shaping his world. We have also seen that the power of observation means the ability to perceive opportunities for manipulating others. What reason could Iago have not to avail himself of these opportunities? One might say that he ought radically to *deny* himself and his own nature, not merely to control himself, but it seems questionable whether that demand is really at all coherent.

In a strict sense one could achieve self-denial through one's own efforts only by leaning on or mobilizing something within oneself, thereby actually affirming oneself at the same time one is denying oneself. Thus self-denial would at the same time prove to be self-affirmation, that is, its own opposite. To the extent to which self-denial is a real possibility, Iago is not an agent who would be capable of carrying it out because he lacks an appropriate inner richness.

This connection is clearly seen in the difficulty that appears on closer inspection of an image used by Iago, which at first sight seems quite obvious and which recalls his remarks about a good reputation:

> Virtue? a fig! 'tis in ourselves, that we are thus, or thus: our bodies are gardens, to the which our wills are gardeners, so that if we will plant nettles, or sow lettuce, set hyssop, and weed up thyme . . . (1.3.320–22)

Perhaps our bodies really are the gardens of our wills. But then who makes our will? If it is true that we can do what we will, but not will what we will, then Iago's *fate*—and therefore not simply his *guilt*—is to have the will that he has. This is not to say that guilt and innocence are always a matter of the will. Perhaps there really is a dimension of guilt in which the decisive thing is only what we do, not what or how we will or do not will. (Oedipus, once again.) Here, however, we are faced precisely with a dimension in which the will does matter. (Iago is no Oedipus.)

Since it is not logically possible, we cannot simply demand self-denial, and the moment Iago appears as a moral subject, like each of us, he proves to be what he is. That alone is what concerns and enables us to defend Iago without justifying him.

38. To repeat, it is an open question how concept and apology, is and ought, understanding and evaluation, relate to each other. Here is another point at which the same problem reemerges. In relation to the two previous sections we might question how Iago can be a villain, if he is distinguished by nothing more than a zest for life embodied in a zest for action, albeit in an exaggerated form. Or we might voice the same objection by asking the prag-

matic question what difference it would make to our deal-
ings with Iago if we followed the idea presented here or,
alternatively, one of the other usual interpretations of his
character.

Bloom, to take issue with him once more, believes that
Iago would not have had a chance if he had encountered a
character such as Falstaff, rather than Othello or Cassio.
As Bradley said about Hamlet, Falstaff would have seen
through Iago immediately. If Iago had been seen through
immediately, many things for which he can be held responsible would not have happened. For our part, we
would have lost the play itself and with it the insights it
offers us. Does the play, then, ultimately work because
Shakespeare has surrounded Iago with somewhat weak
characters?

Where Hamlet is concerned, it is his skepticism that
would forearm him against Iago. As an addiction, this
strength of Hamlet is essentially also his weakness. It
would appear as a strength only if Hamlet were to meet
an Iago—in which case it would actually *be* a strength. But
that new play, in which Hamlet meets Iago, would not
show us what we can learn by reflecting on Hamlet in his
real surroundings. To that extent it is an advantage that
the two never meet. The play about the Prince of Den-
mark therefore raises a question very similar to that raised
by *Othello*. To find an answer, we may fruitfully explore
the implications of the idea that Falstaff would not fall
for Iago's trickery.

We could certainly say that Falstaff derived his defense
against Iago from his insight into the diversity of what
may be called "human passions," including those variants that could be described as "pathological." While it is
possible to argue about Hamlet, it should be obvious that

Falstaff's wisdom, his philosophical vein, his resemblance to Machiavelli, so to speak, would have allowed him to see through Iago. If Bloom suggests that the only defense against Iago is humor, and that Falstaff would simply have laughed Iago off, we must add that this laughter would have been the kind of laughter attributed to the sage, which is the opposite of the sense of the uncanny referred to by Heidegger.

One appropriate reaction to the possibility of Iago, as an incarnation of evil, would, then, be to adopt a philosophical stance to life in general. But of course this reaction is not realistic for those who must *act* in the human world, because laughter such as Falstaff's arises at the moment when we withdraw from life, contemplating it from the outside without intervening, and observing it without reference to a possible intervention. Certainly, Falstaff suffers no less than any other person in his position, that is, no less than we would suffer if we were involved with his prince and king. But he suffers only insofar as he is *one of us*. He, however, is also a highly unusual figure. It is his strength relative to Iago that distinguishes him from run-of-the-mill people like the rest of us: Falstaff's ability to move from an everyday attitude to another attitude altogether sets him apart from us ordinary people. This connects him with Iago, although in his case it is accompanied by a different mentality and temperament. But his quasi-metaphysical perspective does not simply release him from suffering, as a drug, a compensatory moral relief, in short, anything that generally relieves suffering, could do. Rather, its salient feature is that it provides no room for suffering, or, if it does, the suffering is of a different kind. It is the love of which Shakespeare speaks in *Love's Labour's Lost* that characterizes Falstaff. This love is not simply ousted by the suffering that the prince, having become king, inflicts on him; rather, the suffering itself assumes metaphysical features.

Even though everyone has the requisite abilities, we cannot all become philosophers, if it is the withdrawal into contemplation and reflection, rather than intervention in the events, that makes a person a philosopher. The kind of quarantine that Iago would enter if he lived in a group of Falstaffs, therefore, cannot be a general condition. That is why this reaction to the possibility of an Iago cannot be a practicable one. If I am asked the pragmatic question what difference it makes whether or not we follow the interpretation presented here, my answer is that the question has come too late. Those who understand the interpretation automatically assume an attitude that no longer allows them to regard Iago simply as a villain, because that judgment is not part of a purely contemplative attitude.

If, then, there is a practicable reaction to the possibility of Iago, it must be sought in ordinary life. We actually find one if we take a look at Iago's downfall.

2.3. WHY IAGO PERISHES, AND WHAT HIS DOWNFALL MEANS

39. What role does the downfall of Iago (and accordingly of Othello) play from a perspective in which Iago is not simply a villain? This role is revealed by the *manner* of Iago's downfall.

The difference between someone whose downfall is caused by his own guilt, on the one hand, and Iago, on the other, does not consist in something that is completely missing in Iago. On the contrary, there is nothing in Iago that we do not find in everyone, including ourselves, albeit—if we are normal—not in the extravagant, pathological, and therefore pure and extreme form it takes in his case. We could be said to be "substantially" at one with him; with regard to the form that this substance can take, however, the difference is a serious one. The form, to be sure, is not simply external to the substance. Insofar as that form which is particularly appropriate to the substance is the "normal" form, the pathological has no existence of its own or, as I said before, the pathological is defined as a deviation from the healthy. Thus, to some extent, it is not defined by reference to itself. This in turn means that by contemplating the pathological—more accurately, the moment a thing, a condition, a quality, a process, becomes pathological—we learn something about the limits of the normal.[10] These limits are of a conceptual kind. They are revealed durably, clearly, and firmly by what is called "pathological" in comparison to

[10] The pathological method comes in many forms: for Austin as a "theory of infelicities," while Heidegger talks about the modes of conspicuousness, intrusiveness, and rebelliousness of what is at hand—modes in which things do not run as is fitting for them. See Austin's second lecture in *How to Do Things with Words*, ed. M. Sbisa and J. O. Urmson, 2nd ed. (Cambridge, MA: Harvard University Press, 1975), and "A Plea for Excuses," in *Philosophical Papers*, ed. J. O. Urmson and G. J. Warnock, 3rd ed. (Oxford: Oxford University Press, 1979), pp. 175–204; and *Sein und Zeit, Erste Hälfte*, 6th ed. (Tübingen: Neomarius, 1949), § 16, pp. 72ff. (*Being and Time*, trans. John Macquarrie and Edward Robinson [Oxford: Blackwell, 1962], pt. 1, sec. 16, pp. 102ff.) Earlier I mentioned Bloom's remark about war's being Iago's real element (section 12). Erasmus, in *Querela Pacis* (Basel: Froben, 1517), not only calls war the root of all evil, but also sees it as something like a disease, a pathological form of human life. This is then transferred to those whose true element it is.

the normal. This durability informs the effect that the sight of Iago (and, more weakly, of Othello) has on us. The clarity and firmness of the concept displayed through this vision is what I wanted to bring out in a pure form in this study.

Thus the tendency to deny *Othello* a philosophical element, and to understand it instead as a study in psychopathology, is not simply wrong. Rather, it betrays a failure to recognize the philosophical relevance of the pathological. Contemplating (the image of) a perverse person, for example, does not make us doubt morality, but it draws our attention to the limits of the moral, and thus to the limits of what can be justified or condemned. That is what the contemplation of Iago shows us. Iago teaches us our moral limits by transcending them.

A pathology of the moral at the same time shows us in what way the moral is natural. Iago is an unnatural monster, almost in the sense in which a singing adder would be unnatural. In this light, the downfall of Iago displays, in time and space, for all to see, the inherent insubstantiality of his "form" of life: for conceptual reasons it lacks independent subsistence.

40. In this context it is particularly ironic that Iago's scheme should be uncovered by Emilia, of all people, who seems so innocent, almost simpleminded, to Iago that he hardly notices her. For Iago, Emilia represents no really recalcitrant material that he could find any satisfaction in shaping to his will. She does what she does because she is committed to what is customary. For her, keeping her heart to herself while being involved with others is no contradiction. Other people are close to her heart. If the two things are at all different, she sees so little contrast

between them that she is literally prepared to perish for the good reputation of others. Thus she confirms what I said earlier: that a good reputation constitutes our humanity, and to the extent to which it is destroyed, our humanity will also be destroyed. Emilia perishes when those to whom she is bound by her heart see their reputation destroyed. We do not need Shakespeare to observe this phenomenon. We can see time and again how people cease to be themselves when they lose someone to whom, be it physically or morally, their heart belongs. Literally belongs, we would like to add.

Nor does Emilia simply give up, lose herself to the others, wear her heart on her sleeve, so that it can be picked up by them. It is Iago who pierces it, not "the others." The others are as normal as Emilia herself. Emilia is certainly no great figure in whom pure and strong moral forces struggle with each other. She is possibly somewhat childish, and certainly immature. But at the same time she is genuinely human. That is what earns her our respect. The meaning of this respect becomes clear precisely through her simple temperament: she does not measure her strength against Iago's, as Falstaff or Hamlet might have done, but simply confronts him with her pure fellow humanity.[11]

In contrast, Iago's absolute attitude of I-stand-for-myself-alone is either an impossibility, if we understand "I" to mean that there cannot be another *possible* "I" besides himself, because then the complement "and-for-

---

[11] On simplemindedness see Meister Eckhart's "Beati pauperes spiritu," in *Deutsche Predigten und Traktate*, ed. and trans. J. Quint (Zürich: Diogenes Verlag, 1979), pp. 303–9. See also the remark above about the naturalness of trusting others (sections 9 and 27).

no-others" will fall by the wayside; or it is pathological, in that it tries to negate the one thing that can give it a purpose.

Emilia is neither an impossibility nor pathological. She is truthful, or normal, because she is attached to others, and she is attached to others because she is faithful to herself. Indeed, she is attached to others with her whole heart. That is the human standard. But it is an inherent part of that standard that it be potentially transcended. The standard is validated by what conforms to it as much as by what transcends it. In this conceptual connection lies the possibility of a defense of Iago that is not a justification.

Acknowledgments

THERE are some duties that prove—in the process of feeling and, even more, of fulfilling them—that not all duties must necessarily go against the inclinations. One of these is the duty to give thanks.

In the present case the duties stem from various quarters. The first version of this text was a sequel to a lecture about Shakespeare's *King Lear* that I had the privilege of giving at a conference on the philosophy of Stanley Cavell at the Goethe-Universität Frankfurt (am Main). My work on that topic, stimulated by a variety of factors, eventually gave rise to my examination of *Othello*. Subsequently, the first version of this text was discussed in my seminar for advanced students. I can no longer tell how many versions this text has now gone through, but I have vivid memories of several occasions on which I was able to discuss the topics treated in my text with friends and colleagues. These discussions regularly led to further changes in the text. This does not mean that the text got steadily better, but since it is up to the author what, if any, changes he wishes to make, his opportunities to shift the blame to others are limited. However, that does not curtail his duty to thank.

I would like to fulfill this duty toward those who (in very different ways) have helped me arrive at this version. To name some of them, they included José-Maria Arisó, Frank Dietrich, Richard Eldridge, Christoph Fehige, Peter Fischer, Fabian Freyenhagen, Jane Heal, Peter Heuer, Bettina Kremberg, Martin Kusch, Andreas Luckner, Georg Meggle, Ulrich Müller, above all Raymond Geuss and Christoph Menke, Maria Isabel Peña Aguado, Jörg Schaub, Hans-Bernhard Schmid, Mark Siebel, Christian Skirke, Manuela Sorge, Henning Tegtmeyer, Alessandro Tomassini, Max Urchs, and Ulla Wessels.

I am very grateful to the German Research Council which awarded me a Heisenberg Grant. For a philosopher, a Heisenberg is as close to Heaven as it gets on Earth. In my case, it allowed me to work on various manuscripts in peace and tranquillity at the Universities of Heidelberg, Leipzig, and Potsdam. I am also particularly grateful to the Department of History and Philosophy of Science and to the Faculty of Philosophy of the University of Cambridge and to Clare Hall, Cambridge, for providing me with such excellent facilities to pursue my research in congenial circumstances.

Since even in Heaven one needs some help from time to time, thanks are also due to Ladislaus Löb for the translation of the German original. Finally, I want to thank Ian Malcolm of the Princeton University Press for his deep interest in the project as well as his strong support and great patience during its final realization.

Index

aims, realization of, 93–94
Anscombe, Elizabeth, 86
apologia, for Iago, 2, 6–7, 8, 77–107.
    See also defense; justification
appearance, 29; and reality, 24, 31
audience, 12, 27–28, 32, 76; hatred
    of for Iago, 47–48, 79
Augustine, St., 87, 88
Austin, J. L., 85–86, 104n10

Bianca, 40
Bloom, Harold, 26, 27, 28, 70n17,
    74, 81, 101, 102, 104n10
Bradley, A. C., 19, 22, 70n17, 94, 101
Brecht, Bertolt, 59; *Arbeitsjournal*,
    56; "The Friends," 64; *The
    Private Life of the Master Race*, 34;
    Señora Carrar's Rifles, 48

Carrar, Señora, 48
Cassio: and Falstaff, 101; Iago as
    different from, 73; and Iago's
    hatred over preferment, 16; and
    Iago's motive, 14, 18, 20; Othello
    as different from, 40, 73; and
    reputation, 53–54, 55, 74–75;
    role of, 12; and wooing of
    Desdemona, 41
Cavell, Stanley, 42n11
Coleridge, Samuel Taylor, 30–31

concepts: and proper names, 2–4;
    relational, 22, 23, 35, 92
condemnation, 84, 85, 86, 105
conspirator, 59, 64–65
crime, disposition to, 55

defense: and accusation, 78; of Iago,
    84–85, 89, 91–103; and justifica-
    tion, 12–13, 77–78, 79, 85, 86; and
    understanding, 7. *See also* apologia,
    for Iago
de la Rochefoucault, François, 92
Desdemona: Cassio's wooing of, 41;
    and Iago's motive, 18; and mar-
    riage consummation, 41; and
    Othello as absorbed in others,
    39–40; role of, 12; and skin shade,
    28; as title character, 3
destiny, 13, 63
devil, 14, 27, 70
drama: interpretation of, 28; as kind
    of logic, 36; and morality/ethics,
    8–10
dramatic action, 34

Eckhart, Meister, 106n11
egoism, 1–2, 98–99; defined, 11
Emilia: death of, 17; and Iago's
    downfall, 105–7; and Iago's mo-
    tive, 17; Iago's murder of, 17, 21;